CLASSIC THAI CUISINE

Classic Thai Cuisine

David Thompson

TEN SPEED PRESS
Berkeley, California

To Tanongsak

TEN SPEED PRESS
P.O. Box 7123
Berkeley, CA 94707

First published in Australasia in 1993 by
Simon & Schuster Australia
20 Barcoo Street, East Roseville NSW 2069

A Paramount Communications Company
Sydney New York London Toronto Tokyo Singapore

Cover design by Helen Semmler
Text design by Helen Semmler
Additional illustrations by Jan Gosewinckel on pages 8-9, 28-29
Typeset in Australia by Asset Typesetting Pty Ltd

Library of Congress Cataloging-in-Publication Data

Thompson, David
    Classic Thai cuisine / David Thompson; illustrated by Helen Semmler.

        p.   cm.
    British ed. has title: The top one hundred Thai dishes.
    Includes index.
    ISBN 0-89815-563-0
    1. Cookery, Thai. I. Title.
TX724.5.T5T49 1993
641.59593—dc20   93-1770
                                                                  CIP

FIRST PRINTING 1993
Produced by Mandarin Offset
Printed and bound in China

2 3 4 5 — 97 96 95 94

CONTENTS

INTRODUCTION

WAT PRA GAEW in Bangkok's Royal Temple complex is widely regarded as the pinnacle of Thai architecture, design and art — the kaleidoscopic mosaic of form, texture and colour astounds and almost beggars description. Huge Chinese temple guardians and delicate garuda, golds and azures, terracotta and faïence, compete for attention. Gorgeous and opulent, rich and truly exotic, its beauty might bewilder and overwhelm. However, such is the genius of the Thais that they have wielded these components into one of the world's most extraordinary and harmonious buildings. In another culture what could have been glittering gaudy becomes, with the Thai sense of balance, enticingly beautiful. I see many parallels in Thai food: complexities of flavour and intricate textures that in any other cuisine would confuse and exhaust the palate seem only to delight and scintillate.

This remarkable cuisine is a paradox: chillies, garlic, ginger, fish sauce, palm sugar, lime and lemongrass, the staples of Thai cooking are robustly flavoured ingredients. Yet they are melded and tempered by one another into an elegant, refined finish, in which no one flavour is either overpowered or dominant. At the same time, their flavours are further intensified by the use of seasonings so that sweet, sour, salty and hot are contrasted. The resulting depth of flavour and balance of seasoning produces a clarity, a vitality of taste that in Thai is called *rot chart*, proper harmony of flavour. It is the epitome of Thai cuisine.

In their cuisine as in their architecture, the Thais are renowned for their skill in decoration, especially in fruit and vegetable carving. Delicate and engaging though it is, were it not for the Thais' consistent commitment to quality and sound technique throughout all of the processes of cooking — from choosing the produce, to the preparation, the cooking process, seasonings and presentation — such embellishments could become mere ostentation. Instead they seem the perfect final expression of diligence and care, encapsulating the Thai saying *gan gin gan yuu*, as you eat, so you are. It is an axiom which parallels Brillat-Savarin's 'You are what you eat', but suggests further that not only are you what you eat, you also define yourself by the manner in which you approach food — the choice of ingredients, their preparation and their presentation are all indicative of what you are. And in this the Thais acquit themselves very well indeed.

Rice is at the core of Thai cuisine. The Thais are an agricultural people, their lives bound inextricably to the rice-growing cycle. In the country, daily existence revolves around the cultivation of rice, and everywhere traditions and ritual recall and celebrate this consuming relationship the Thais have had with the grain over the centuries. To waste it is to disregard its benefice. Even today, after finishing a meal, young Thais will often raise their hands in a respectful gesture to the rice, acknowledging their gratitude to this staff of life.

A proper meal is inconceivable without it. All other dishes, curries, salads, whatever else is on the table, are called *gap kao*, with rice. All wet dishes serve to dress and moisten the rice, making it more palatable. All dry dishes add texture, making it more interesting. It is, however, the rice that is being consumed, that is the sustenance. Any other dish, no matter how attractive and delicious, merely acts as its condiment. In a Thai meal, the normal proportion of rice to other dishes is 3:2.

There is no set order of progression to a Thai meal — all main course dishes are served at once — although there must be a balance of flavours and textures in the individual dishes, and between each dish, so that repetition is avoided. The contrasting tastes and textures of dry, wet, sour, sweet, hot, mild and crisp, soft combine to make up the Thai meal. A Hot and Sour Soup goes perfectly with a *Lon*; a Sour Orange Curry is delicious with Salty Beef and Steamed Eggs; and a *Nam Prik* complements the Omelette Soup. Part of the delight in a Thai meal is the myriad combinations that can be wrought.

Normally, when the Thais eat they allow one savoury dish per person plus rice. The more people there are to dine, the greater the variety of dishes — and Thais, being social creatures, love to eat with a crowd. The recipes in this book cater for up to six people. For greater numbers it would be wise to increase the quantities in the recipes accordingly. If there are fewer people, rather than having two or three dishes, decrease the quantities in the recipes and increase the variety so that there are four or five dishes.

The Thai table is very flexible, and the only firm rule is that the food should be served in a friendly and relaxed atmosphere. The generosity and hospitality of the host is reflected not in the richness of the dishes or the variety of the table, but in the enjoyment and pleasure of entertaining.

APPETISERS, SNACKS AND NOODLES

Appetisers, Snacks and Noodles

THAIS ARE INVETERATE snackers. Throughout Thailand, throughout the day — a fish cake here, some spring rolls there — Thais snack. Near schools and office blocks, anywhere near people, there are always food vendors who cater for this favoured national pastime.

Usually only one main meal is eaten a day, and this is always accompanied by rice. Everything else that the Thais eat is either snacks or noodles — in fact by some perverse logic, snacks are not even considered real food, merely a pleasant diversion to while away any spare time. Food, and snacks especially, is an entertainment to the Thais, albeit a serious one. Often hours are spent discussing the merits of one dish as opposed to another and great consternation occurs when a dish seems to be ineptly produced.

Noodles are traditionally eaten at lunchtime, or when one is in a rush or eating alone. They are one of the few foods that are not shared and they are always served with condiments — *kreuang brung* — that enable the noodles to be seasoned as desired. *Kanom jin* are very unusual noodles which often take the place of rice at lunchtime. They are made from rice flour and are highly perishable — although perversely, they are a propitious food that symbolises good fortune and long life.

Thai food is not an arrogant cuisine in that it does not demand stringent adherence to recipes or that a dish must be seasoned and finished in one way, and one way alone. It allows for individual choice. Most recipes conclude with the instructions *brung tam chorp jai*, season to your liking. In older recipes, quantities were seldom given for ingredients as it was assumed that dishes would be seasoned and flavoured according to experience and preference. The Thais believe that each cook has a predisposition to one of the four basic seasonings, hot, sweet, sour or salty, and so will season accordingly.

PRAWNS WRAPPED IN GREEN LEAVES
Miang Gung

10 betel, spinach or *butter lettuce*
leaves, rinsed and dried
½ *lime, unpeeled, cut into small*
cubes
5 *red shallots, cubed*
3 *cm (1¼ in) piece young ginger,*
cubed
5 *small fresh red or green chillies,*
finely sliced
2 *tablespoons peanuts, roasted and*
coarsely ground
2 *tablespoons fresh coconut,*
shredded and roasted
½ *stalk lemongrass, finely sliced*
100 *g (4 oz) small prawns*
(shrimp), peeled and deveined

MIANG SAUCE
1 *tablespoon galangal, peeled,*
shredded and roasted (see
glossary)
2 *tablespoons dried prawns*
(shrimp)
3 *tablespoons grated fresh coconut,*
roasted
2 *teaspoons kapi (shrimp paste),*
roasted (see glossary)
1 *cup palm sugar*
60 *mL (4 tablespoons) fish sauce*
250 *mL (1 cup/8 fl oz) water*

THIS DISH REFLECTS the wonderful interplay of
flavours and textures that make up Thai food. Here
the chilli is counterbalanced by the ginger and the
lime which cuts the sweetness from the palm sugar.
As an interesting, although less authentic,
alternative, smoked trout with salmon roe could be
used instead of the prawns.

To make this a vegetarian dish, omit the dried and
fresh prawns and kapi, and double the 2 tablespoons
of coconut to 4 tablespoons.

Method: Arrange the green leaves on a serving plate.
Combine the remaining ingredients in a bowl, dress
with 45 mL (3 tablespoons) of the miang sauce and
serve on top of the leaves.

To make the sauce, pound the galangal, dried
prawns, coconut and kapi in a mortar and pestle
(or food processor) until fine. Combine with the
remaining ingredients in a small pan and simmer for
10 minutes until the sauce has reduced by half.
Skim regularly. Strain and cool.

PORK SATAY
Muu Satay

6 red shallots, chopped
1 teaspoon fresh turmeric or
    ½ teaspoon powdered turmeric
1 teaspoon salt
30 mL (2 tablespoons) fish sauce
1 tablespoon palm sugar
500 g (1 lb) pork, cut into
    4 cm x 1 cm (1½ x ½ in) strips

CHILLI PASTE
250 mL (1 cup/8 fl oz) coconut
    cream
7-10 large dried red chillies,
    deseeded and chopped
3 red shallots, chopped
3 cloves garlic
1 stalk lemongrass, sliced
1 tablespoon galangal, peeled and
    chopped
1 teaspoon kaffir lime zest
2 coriander (cilantro) roots
1 teaspoon kapi (shrimp paste),
    roasted (see glossary)
1 tablespoon coriander (cilantro)
    seeds, roasted
1 tablespoon cumin seeds, roasted
1 teaspoon salt

SATAY SAUCE
750 mL (3 cups/1¼ pt) coconut cream
All of the chilli paste
45 mL (3 tablespoons) fish sauce
3 tablespoons sugar
60 mL (4 tablespoons) tamarind
    water (see glossary)
150 g (5 oz) peanuts, roasted and
    ground

THROUGHOUT THAILAND, on the streets and in the markets, there is always a satay stall, with its sweet fragrance beckoning. Satays are grilled over charcoal that impregnates the meat with a smoky flavour. Chicken, beef or prawns may also be used. The Cucumber Relish (see page 14) cuts the richness of the coconut cream in the satay sauce.

Method: In a mortar and pestle (or food processor), pound the shallots, turmeric and salt until fine. Combine in a bowl with the remaining ingredients and marinate overnight.

Soak bamboo skewers in water for 30 minutes. Thread the strips of pork onto the skewers and grill over a low heat or broil, turning and basting with the marinade, for about 5 minutes or until cooked as desired. Serve with the satay sauce and cucumber relish.

To make the chilli paste, purée all of the ingredients in a food processor until fine.

To make the satay sauce, in a medium pan, boil the coconut cream until it separates, about 3-5 minutes. Add the chilli paste and fry for 10 minutes or until fragrant, stirring constantly to prevent the paste and its spices from scorching. Add the fish sauce, sugar and tamarind water, continue to simmer for a further 5 minutes, and then add the peanuts. The glistening sauce will taste equally salty, sweet and sour.

FISH CAKES WITH CUCUMBER RELISH

Tod Man Pla

300 g (10 oz) redfish or red
   snapper fillets
1 quantity chilli paste (see pages
   24-25)
1 egg
45 mL (3 tablespoons) fish sauce
1 teaspoon white (granulated) sugar
5 kaffir lime leaves, shredded
50 g (2 oz) snake (long green)
   beans, finely sliced across
1 L (4 cups/1¾ pt) safflower oil for
   deep-frying

CUCUMBER RELISH
60 mL (4 tablespoons) Thai
   coconut vinegar
4 tablespoons white (granulated)
   sugar
60 mL (4 tablespoons) water
1 coriander (cilantro) root, chopped
   finely
1 head pickled garlic, chopped, and
   its juice (see page 118, optional)
Pinch salt
1 small cucumber, quartered
   lengthways and sliced
4 red shallots, finely sliced
2 tablespoons ginger, julienned
1 long fresh red chilli, julienned
1 tablespoon fresh coriander
   (cilantro) leaves

FISH CAKES ARE fish cakes are fish cakes unless they are Thai fish cakes. Among the most familiar and popular dishes in the Thai repertoire, this snack should always be eaten hot, because when cold or overcooked it has the consistency and appearance of a flat rubber tyre.

Method: Wash the fish in cold salted water and pat dry. Combine the fish, chilli paste, egg, fish sauce and sugar in a food processor, blend well. In a medium bowl, further incorporate the mixture by scooping it up and throwing it back into the bowl several times until it is sticky. Then add the lime leaves and beans. Mould the mixture into disks measuring 5 cm (2 in) in diameter x 0.5 cm (¼ in) thick. In a wok over a medium heat, deep-fry the cakes in the oil for about 4-5 minutes or until golden. Serve the cakes as soon as they have cooked — they toughen as they cool — with the cucumber relish.

To make the cucumber relish, in a small pan combine the vinegar, sugar, water, coriander root, pickled garlic and juice, and salt. Bring to the boil and stir until the sugar dissolves. Remove from the heat. Strain and cool. It will taste sweet and sour. Combine the remaining ingredients in a serving bowl and pour over the vinegar/sugar liquid.

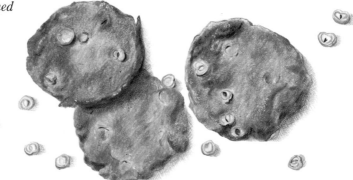

RICE CAKES WITH PORK, PRAWNS AND COCONUT CREAM RELISH

Kao Tang Nan Tang

300 g (2 cups) freshly cooked rice
*1 L (4 cups/1¾ pt) safflower oil for
  deep-frying*

CHILLI PASTE
5 large dried red chillies
4 cloves garlic, chopped
3 coriander (cilantro) roots
10 white peppercorns, ground
1 teaspoon salt

RELISH
*250 mL (1 cup/8 fl oz) coconut
  cream*
All of the chilli paste
45 mL (3 tablespoons) fish sauce
3 tablespoons palm sugar
100 g (4 oz) pork, minced (ground)
*100 g (4 oz) prawns (shrimp),
  minced (ground)*
*250 mL (1 cup/8 fl oz) coconut
  milk*
*2 tablespoons chilli jam (see
  page 85, optional)*
*3 red shallots, finely sliced
  lengthways*
*2 tablespoons peanuts, roasted and
  coarsely ground*
*2 tablespoons coriander (cilantro)
  leaves*

RICE CAKES ARE a classic Thai appetiser. They are easy to make and can be kept almost indefinitely prior to garnishing. Chilli jam with some cooked prawns may be used to garnish the cakes instead.

Method: Firmly press the rice onto a flat metal tray 35 x 25 cm (14 x 10 in). Dry out in a very low oven overnight. When the rice is dry and hard, remove from the tray and store in an airtight container.

To serve, break the rice cakes into bite-sized pieces, then quickly deep-fry them in hot oil for about 1 minute or until they puff, avoid colouring. Turn the cakes over, then remove and drain. Serve accompanied by the relish.

To make the chilli paste, purée the chillies, garlic, coriander roots, peppercorns and salt in a food processor until fine.

To make the relish, in a medium pan, boil the coconut cream until it separates, 3–5 minutes. Add the chilli paste and fry for 5 minutes, stirring regularly, until fragrant. Add the fish sauce, palm sugar, pork and prawns. Fry for a further 2 minutes, then add the coconut milk and simmer for 5 minutes. Add the chilli jam, if using, and check the seasoning. The relish will be sweet and salty. Mix in the shallots and peanuts. Pour into a small serving bowl, sprinkle with the coriander leaves and serve.

SPRING ROLLS

Po Piah Tort

50 g (2 oz) vermicelli noodles
2 cloves garlic
1 coriander (cilantro) root
5 white peppercorns
Pinch salt
15 mL (1 tablespoon) safflower oil
50 g (2 oz) prawn (shrimp) meat,
    minced
50 g (2 oz) pork, minced (ground)
30 mL (2 tablespoons) fish sauce
1 tablespoon palm sugar
100 g (4 oz) bean sprouts, topped
    and tailed
2 tablespoons fresh coriander
    (cilantro) leaves
2 tablespoons sliced Chinese
    shallots
1 packet spring roll wrappers
    (about 50 sheets)
4 tablespoons plain (all-purpose)
    flour mixed with 30 mL
    (2 tablespoons) water to make a
    paste
1.5 L (6 cups/2½ pt) safflower oil
    for deep-frying

THESE ROLLS ARE a perennial favourite of the Thais, who love to snack on them anytime of day. Serve with Cucumber Relish (see page 14).

Method: Soak the noodles in warm water for at least 10 minutes, then drain and cut them into 2 cm (¾ in) lengths with scissors. In a mortar and pestle (or food processor) pound together the garlic, coriander root, peppercorns and salt until fine. In a wok heat the oil over a medium heat and fry the mixture until fragrant. Add the prawns and pork and fry until cooked, about 3 minutes. Add the noodles and then season with the fish sauce and palm sugar. Place the mixture in a bowl, allow to cool, then mix in the bean sprouts, coriander leaves and shallots.

Lay the spring roll wrappers on a board, a few at a time, and place 1 tablespoon of the cooled mixture along the centre of each wrapper. Roll up the bottom edge of the wrapper and then fold over the left and right sides. Roll the wrapper until it has almost reached the top edge. Seal the roll with the flour and water paste. Put aside for 1 hour to allow the paste to dry and seal the rolls.

Heat the oil in a wok to a medium heat and fry 4–5 spring rolls at a time for 5 minutes, or until golden. Remove and drain on paper towels. Serve immediately.

POACHED CHICKEN AND RICE

Kao Man Gai

1 corn-fed chicken
Pinch salt
2 teaspoons water
3 L (5¼ pt) chicken stock
1 tablespoon oyster sauce
1 teaspoon palm sugar
1 knob bruised ginger, about
   2 x 1 cm (¾ x ⅓ in) in size
10–16 fresh coriander (cilantro)
   stalks (reserve the leaves and
   roots for later use in this recipe)
1 waxy gourd, peeled, deseeded and
   roll cut (see glossary)
3 cups jasmine rice
½ cup white sticky rice, soaked
   overnight (see glossary)
4 tablespoons of the rendered
   chicken fat (see method)
3 cloves garlic, crushed with a
   pinch of salt
4 tablespoons fresh coriander
   (cilantro) leaves
10 white peppercorns, ground
3–4 small cucumbers, finely sliced

YELLOW BEAN SAUCE
2 coriander (cilantro) roots,
   scraped and sliced
2 tablespoons Thai yellow bean
   sauce, rinsed
1 tablespoon chopped ginger
22 mL (1½ tablespoons) Thai
   coconut vinegar
15 mL (1 tablespoon) soy sauce
15 mL (1 tablespoon) sweet soy sauce
1 tablespoon castor (superfine) sugar
2 fresh long red chillies, chopped

THE THAIS EAT this often for lunch, or supper, especially when eating alone. Cucumber can be used instead of the gourd.

Method: Wash the chicken and remove all visible fat. Place the fat in a small pan, add the salt and water, and boil until the fat is rendered and the water evaporated. If this does not amount to 4 tablespoons of rendered chicken fat, make up the difference with shallot- or garlic-flavoured oil.

In a large pan combine the stock, oyster sauce and palm sugar. Bring to the boil, then add the ginger and the coriander stalks. Return to the boil, then add the chicken, gourd and enough liquid to just cover the chicken. Poach over a low heat for 30 minutes. Allow the chicken to cool in the stock.

Rinse the rice in several changes of water until the water runs clear. Heat the rendered chicken fat in a medium pan, add the garlic and fry until it begins to colour. Add the rice and fry for 3–4 minutes. Strain enough stock from the poached chicken to cover the rice by 1.5 cm (⅓ in). Bring rapidly to the boil, then turn the heat down and simmer, covered, for about 20 minutes, or until cooked. When ready to serve, spoon onto individual plates.

Remove the chicken from the stock and lift the meat from the bones, slice and lay on top of the rice.

Ladle the soupy stock and gourd into a large bowl, and sprinkle with the coriander leaves and pepper. Arrange the cucumbers on a side plate. Serve the rice and chicken, the soup, and the cucumber accompanied by the yellow bean sauce.

To make the yellow bean sauce, in a mortar and pestle (or food processor) pound together the coriander roots, yellow beans and ginger until very fine. Add the vinegar, soy sauces, sugar and chillies.

GREEN PAWPAW SALAD WITH COCONUT RICE
Som Tam Kao Man Gati

PAWPAW (PAPAYA) SALAD
2 cloves garlic
3-9 small fresh red chillies
Pinch salt
*2 tablespoons dried prawns
    (shrimp)*
*3 cherry (baby) tomatoes, coarsely
    chopped*
*2-3 snake (long green) beans, cut
    into 2 cm (¾ in) lengths*
15 mL (1 tablespoon) fish sauce
2 teaspoons palm sugar
*15-30 mL (1-2 tablespoons) lime
    juice*
*15 mL (1 tablespoon) tamarind
    water (see glossary, optional)*
*2 cups (8 oz) shredded green
    pawpaw (papaya)*
*3-5 small dried red chillies,
    roasted (see glossary)*

COCONUT RICE
2 cups jasmine rice
1 L (4 cups/1¾ pt) coconut milk
*4 tablespoons castor (superfine)
    sugar*
2 washed pandanus leaves

THESE TWO DISHES form an older-style combination that is often eaten for lunch with Sweet Salty Beef. The Green Pawpaw Salad, the famous *Som Tam* from the north-east, is hot, salty and sour. Every province has a different version of this salad — in the north they like to add salted rice-field crabs; in the north-east, rice-field cockroaches. Pawpaw is the most common version of this salad, but cucumber, green mango or pomelo may also be used. The coconut rice is very rich and should only be eaten in small amounts.

Method: In a mortar and pestle (or food processor) pound the garlic, fresh chillies and salt until fine. Add the prawns and continue to pound until the prawns are puréed. Add the tomatoes and the beans and crush coarsely. Add the fish sauce, palm sugar, lime juice and tamarind water. Mix in the pawpaw, lightly crushing it. Garnish with the dried chillies and serve accompanied by the Sweet Salty Beef and coconut rice.

To make the coconut rice, wash the rice in several changes of water until it runs clear. In a medium pan stir the coconut milk, sugar and pandanus leaves over a low heat until the sugar dissolves. Add the rice, cover and bring to the boil. Turn the heat down to very low and simmer, covered, for about 20 minutes, or until the rice is cooked. Turn off the heat and allow the rice to continue steaming in the pan for a further 10 minutes before serving.

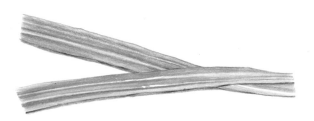

CHIANG MAI NOODLES

Kao Soi

500 mL (2 cups/16 fl oz) coconut cream
All of the curry paste
30 mL (2 tablespoons) thick soy sauce
500 g (1 lb) chicken drumsticks, chopped into thirds
1 L (4 cups/1¾ pt) chicken stock
1 L (4 cups/1¾ pt) safflower oil
2 (375 g/12 oz) packets egg noodles
4 cloves garlic
4 dried long red chillies
Pinch salt
1 teaspoon white (granulated) sugar
3 tablespoons coriander (cilantro) leaves

GARNISH
100 g (4 oz) quartered red shallots
20 fresh coriander (cilantro) leaves
100 g (4 oz) pickled mustard greens, sliced
3 limes, washed and quartered
The chilli and garlic mix
Fresh vegetables, such as green beans, savoy cabbage and fresh Thai basil leaves

CURRY PASTE
5 dried long red chillies, chopped
4 red shallots, chopped
3 cloves garlic
2 coriander (cilantro) roots
1 teaspoon salt
1 tablespoon curry powder (see glossary)

THIS IS A NORTHERN Thai equivalent of Malaysian laksa noodles and is always eaten for lunch. Beef or pork may also be used.

Method: In a medium pan, boil the coconut cream over medium heat, stirring constantly until it separates, 8–10 minutes. Add the curry paste and fry for 2–3 minutes until fragrant. Add the soy sauce and the chicken. Seal the meat then cover with the stock. Simmer until the chicken is tender, about 15 minutes.

Heat the oil in a wok and deep-fry 1 cup of the egg noodles until crisp. Strain and put the crisped noodles to one side. Then reuse 2 tablespoons of that oil to fry the garlic until it begins to colour. Add the dried chillies to the garlic and continue to fry until fragrant. Strain and cool. When the garlic/chilli mix is cooled, pound coarsely in a mortar and pestle (or grinder) with the salt and sugar.

Bring a large pan of salted water to the boil and blanch the remaining egg noodles according to the instructions on the packet. To serve, distribute the noodles equally between 6 individual bowls. Ladle over the chicken curry, then sprinkle with some of the crisped noodles and the coriander. Serve with garnish ingredients arranged on side plates.

To make the curry paste, purée all of the ingredients in a food processor using as little water as possible.

NOODLES WITH PRAWNS AND GARNISHES
Kanom Jin Nam Prik

600 g (1¼ lb) kanom jin or somen
noodles (fine white rice noodles)
200 g (7 oz) prawns (shrimp),
finely chopped
200 mL (1 scant cup/7 fl oz)
coconut milk
1 teaspoon sugar
Pinch salt
4 tablespoons chilli jam (see
page 85)
200 mL (1 scant cup/7 fl oz)
coconut cream
1 tablespoon yellow mung beans,
roasted, peeled and ground
(optional)
30 mL (2 tablespoons) fish sauce
15 mL (1 tablespoon) tamarind
water (see glossary)
2 tablespoons palm sugar
15 mL (1 tablespoon) kaffir lime juice
15 mL (1 tablespoon) lime juice,
increase by 1 tablespoon if the
kaffir lime juice is unobtainable
3 cloves garlic, sliced and deep-
fried until golden (see glossary)
2 tablespoons Chinese shallots
2 tablespoons coriander leaves,
chopped

GARNISHES
½ small green pawpaw (papaya),
peeled and julienned
1 banana blossom, shredded (see
glossary)
10 large dried red chillies, deep-
fried for 1 minute

THE COMPLEXITY AND character of Thai food lie in the interlayering and contrasting of flavours and textures typical of this dish — while the central curry is quite simple, the garnishes and side dishes make this a most regal meal. This recipe appears in an early anthology of Thai food by Princess Yaowaparpongsanit, and comes from a period when labour and time were the least considered components in the kitchen. It is not necessary to reproduce this meal in its entirety — recently in Bangkok I had the curry, the noodles and some fresh vegetables from this compilation — but as a whole it indicates the intricate and highly sophisticated nature of Thai food.

Method: Blanch and refresh the noodles according to the instructions on the packet. Reheat them gently in a steamer. Meanwhile in a small pan, bring the prawns, coconut milk, sugar and salt to the boil, reduce heat and simmer until the prawns are cooked, about 2 minutes. Allow to cool, then strain, reserving the prawns and milk for later use.

Pound the cooked prawns with the chilli jam until fine.

In another small pan, bring to the boil the coconut cream. Stirring constantly over a high heat, add the prawns and chilli jam mixture and mung bean flour and cook for 4 minutes until the colour of the paste deepens and becomes fragrant. Moisten with the reserved coconut milk, then add the fish sauce, tamarind water, palm sugar, kaffir lime juice and lime juice. It will taste sour, salty and sweet.

CRISP PRAWN (SHRIMP) CAKES
200 g (7 oz) very small green
* prawns (raw shrimp), peeled*
2 tablespoons rice flour
1 teaspoon salt
4 tablespoons batter (see page 25)
1 L (4 cups/1¾ pt) safflower oil

FISH CAKES
⅓ recipe (see page 14)

PRAWN (SHRIMP) CAKES
1 clove garlic
1 coriander (cilantro) root
5 white peppercorns
1 teaspoon salt
200 g (7 oz) small prawns (shrimp),
* peeled and finely chopped*
1 teaspoon white (granulated) sugar
1 teaspoon fish sauce

STIR-FRIED VEGETABLES
(see page 93)

5 hardboiled duck or chicken eggs,
* peeled and halved*

Fresh vegetables such as green
* beans and cucumber*

COCONUT CREAM SAUCE
100 mL (½ cup/4 fl oz) coconut cream
100 mL (½ cup/4 fl oz) coconut milk
1 clove garlic, crushed with
* 1 coriander (cilantro) root,*
* 5 white peppercorns and pinch*
* salt*
100 g (4 oz) chicken, finely minced
* (ground)*
30 mL (2 tablespoons) fish sauce
1 teaspoon palm sugar

DEEP-FRIED BANANAS
(see page 128)

Divide the noodles between 6 individual bowls, top with the prawns and chilli jam paste. Sprinkle with the deep-fried garlic, the sliced Chinese shallots and the coriander. Serve with the garnish ingredients, sauce and side dishes of your choice.

To make the crisp prawn cakes, combine all of the ingredients and make into small disks about 2.5 cm (1 in) in diameter. In a wok or deep-frier, heat the oil, add the prawn disks and cook for 5 minutes, or until golden. Strain the oil and reserve for frying the fish cakes. The prawn cakes are used for flavour and textural contrast — so while it may be overcooked to Western standards it is correct and appropriate for this dish.

To make the prawn cakes, in a mortar and pestle (or in a food processor), pound the garlic, coriander root, white peppercorns and salt. When well puréed, add the prawns and continue to pound until the mixture is sticky, then season with the sugar and fish sauce. Mould into small disks 2.5 cm (1 in) in diameter then deep-fry in the oil for 5 minutes, or until golden.

To make the coconut cream sauce, in a small pan, bring the coconut cream and coconut milk to the boil over a medium heat. Add the garlic, coriander and peppercorn mixture. When this has dissolved add the chicken, stirring constantly to prevent clumping. After 3 minutes, season with the fish sauce and palm sugar. Do not overcook the chicken as it will toughen.

NOODLES WITH PINEAPPLE AND PRAWNS
Kanom Jin Sao Nam

600 g (1¼ lb) kanom jin *or* somen
    noodles (fine white rice noodles)
125 mL (½ cup/4 fl oz) fish sauce
125 mL (½ cup/4 fl oz) lime juice
3-4 tablespoons palm sugar
10-20 small fresh red or green
    chillies
½ small pineapple, finely chopped
½ cup dried prawns (shrimp),
    pounded or ground
3 cloves garlic, finely sliced
½ cup julienned young ginger
3 hardboiled eggs, shelled and
    quartered

COCONUT CREAM SAUCE
2 cloves garlic, chopped
2 coriander (cilantro) roots,
    chopped
10 white peppercorns
1 teaspoon salt
15 mL (1 tablespoon) water
250 mL (1 cup/8 fl oz) coconut
    cream
250 mL (1 cup/8 fl oz) coconut
    milk
30 mL (2 teaspoons) fish sauce
1 teaspoon white (granulated)
    sugar
200 g (7 oz) redfish, red snapper,
    ling, or swordfish, *finely*
    chopped

THESE NOODLES ARE much less complex than the preceding recipe and would be delicious for a summer's lunch. Fresh prawns may be substituted for the dried ones. This lunchtime dish is often served with a *Jeng Rorn* (sauce) such as the one given here.

Method: Blanch and refresh the noodles according to the instructions on the packet. Reheat them gently in a steamer. Meanwhile combine the fish sauce, lime juice, palm sugar and chillies. This dressing will taste sour, salty and sweet, and is very hot and pungent.

To serve, divide the noodles between 6 individual plates, and top with the pineapple, ground prawns, garlic and ginger. Drizzle about 30 mL (2 tablespoons) of the sauce over each plate, reserving a little for those who prefer their noodles even hotter. Garnish with the eggs on the side.

To make the coconut cream sauce, in a mortar and pestle (or food processor) crush the garlic, coriander roots, peppercorns and salt until fine, then stir in the water. In a medium pan, heat the combined coconut cream and milk until boiling, then stir in the garlic/peppercorn mix, fish sauce and sugar. Add the fish and cook for 2-3 minutes. Check that the taste is salty and slightly sweet, adding more fish sauce and/or sugar if necessary.

RICE WITH PRAWN PASTE

Kao Kluk Kapi

30 mL (2 tablespoons) safflower oil
    in which garlic has been deep-
    fried
1 teaspoon kapi (shrimp paste),
    roasted (see glossary)
15 mL (1 tablespoon) stock
150 g (1 cup/7 oz) rice, freshly
    cooked but not too hot
2 cloves garlic, sliced lengthways
    and deep-fried (see glossary)
2 tablespoons deep-fried dried
    prawns (shrimp)
4 red shallots, sliced
½ small green mango, julienned
1 quantity Sweet Pork (see page
    120)
1 one-egg omelette, finely sliced
3 Salty Eggs (see page 116),
    quartered
4–8 fresh small green chillies

GARNISH
Finely sliced fresh vegetables such
    as 1 medium head of young
    ginger, 1 cucumber and 50 g
    (2 oz) savoy cabbage, coriander
    (cilantro) sprigs and Chinese
    shallots

THIS WAS A FAVOURITE dish of King Chulalongkorn (Rama V) who reigned from 1868 to 1910. It was during his reign that Siam opened up to the West, and through his diplomatic ability (and the Western need for a buffer state between the two great imperialist powers of south-eastern Asia) that Siam remained a sovereign state, the only uncolonised state in the region. During this time Thai food reached unprecedented heights of refinement, and court food was most elaborate, as exemplified by Princess Yaowaparpongsanit's *Kanom Jin* (Noodles with Prawns and Chilli Jam). Yet the King, at the pinnacle of society, most able to partake of these fruits, preferred a simpler, more frugal cuisine. He enjoyed *Nam Prik Kapi* (Prawn Paste Relish) — as do all Thais — and this following dish, in which many simple and strong flavours enhance and delight in their combination rather than confuse and cloy.

Method: Heat the oil in a wok, add the kapi and fry for 2–3 minutes or until fragrant. Add the stock. Mix in the warm rice. Serve garnished with the remaining ingredients.

PERFUMED RICE WITH GARNISHES
Kao Chae

RICE
300 g (10 oz) jasmine rice
some cracked ice
10 Thai jasmine flowers or rose
petals, steeped for no less than
4 hours and no more than
24 hours in 500 mL
(2 cups/16 fl oz) water

STUFFED BANANA CHILLIES
10 small banana chillies or
capsicums (peppers)
1 clove garlic
2 coriander (cilantro) roots
10 white peppercorns
1 teaspoon salt
150 g (5 oz) green prawns (raw
shrimp), deveined and chopped
100 g (4 oz) pork, minced (ground)
2 tablespoons peanuts, roasted and
ground
1 egg
30 mL (2 tablespoons) fish sauce
1 tablespoon castor (superfine)
sugar

STUFFED SHALLOTS
CHILLI PASTE
3 red shallots, chopped (see main
method)
3 dried red long chillies, deseeded
and chopped
2 cloves garlic
1 stalk lemongrass
1 teaspoon galangal, peeled and
chopped

KAO CHAE WAS devised during the reign of King Rama V to revive flagging palates during the hot summer months. In its original form, *Kao Chae* was simply cold rice in jasmine-scented water served with salty beef and fresh vegetables. In this elaborate version, sound technique is required. Not all garnishes are essential, so choose as preferred. If you find it too daunting to make the chilli paste for the stuffed shallots, you can use any leftover red curry paste — as long as it doesn't contain too much dried spice. This chilli paste can be used in both *Tort Man Pla* (Fish Cakes, see page 14) or the *Hor Mawk* (Steamed Fish Curry, see page 60).

Method: Wash the rice in several changes of water, then soak in salted water for 2–3 hours. Parboil the rice in plenty of salted water for 1 minute, then refresh. Repeat this process three more times. This helps to remove the starch from the rice so that the grains become quite shiny. Finally, steam the rice for about 5 minutes, or until cooked. Allow to cool before serving. Spoon the rice into 6 individual bowls and top with cracked ice and jasmine or rose-scented water. This rice is served with the following accompaniments.

To make the stuffed banana chillies, wash the chillies, then remove the tops (retain) and, using a small knife, remove the seeds and connective membranes. Wash again to remove all the seeds.

In a mortar and pestle (or food processor) pound together the garlic, coriander roots, peppercorns and salt until fine. In a bowl mix together the chopped prawns, pork, garlic mixture, peanuts and egg. Add the fish sauce and sugar.

1 coriander (cilantro) root

1 teaspoon kaffir lime zest

*1 teaspoon kapi (shrimp paste),
roasted (see glossary)*

10 white peppercorns, ground

20 large red shallots

*250 mL (1 cup/8 fl oz) coconut
cream*

3 tablespoons of the chilli paste

*1 cup dried prawns (shrimp),
ground*

*1 teaspoon while (granulated)
sugar*

1 teaspoon fish sauce (optional)

*1 L (4 cups/1¾ pt) safflower oil for
deep-frying*

FRYING BATTER

*1 cup (4 oz) plain (all-purpose)
flour*

2 tablespoons rice flour

1 teaspoon salt

*1 tablespoon castor (superfine)
sugar*

1 tablespoon baking powder

30 mL (2 tablespoons) safflower oil

250 mL (1 cup/8 fl oz) water

PRAWN (SHRIMP) PASTE BALLS

*2 cups smoked trout or slow-grilled
catfish*

4 red shallots, chopped

3 tablespoons krachai (see glossary)

1 stalk lemongrass, sliced

*3 tablespoons grated coconut,
roasted*

*3 tablespoons kapi (shrimp paste),
roasted (see glossary)*

30 mL (2 tablespoons) safflower oil

1 tablespoon palm sugar

30 mL (2 tablespoons) fish sauce

Stuff the chillies with this mixture and replace the tops. Steam the chillies for about 10 minutes, or until cooked. Serve warm.

To make the chilli paste for the stuffed shallots, in a food processor, purée all of the ingredients from the 3 shallots to the white peppercorns and as little water as possible, until fine.

Peel the shallots, slice off their tops and remove the insides with a teaspoon. They can be used for the chilli paste or for prawn paste balls.

Place half the coconut cream in a small pan, and heat until it separates, 3–5 minutes. Add the chilli paste and fry for 2–3 minutes until fragrant. Add the prawns, remaining coconut cream, sugar and fish sauce. Simmer, stirring constantly for about 10 minutes or until the mixture is quite sticky. Allow to cool then stuff the shallots with this mixture. Heat the oil in a wok, dip the shallots in the frying batter, then deep-fry for about 5 minutes, or until golden.

To make the frying batter, sift the flours with the salt into a bowl, then whisk in the other ingredients. Let stand for 1 hour before using. The batter should give a thin, rather than a thick, coating. It may be necessary to add some extra water if it is too thick.

To make the prawn paste balls, in a food processor purée the fish, shallots, krachai, lemongrass, coconut and kapi until fine. Heat safflower oil in a small pan, add the purée and fry for about 2–3 minutes, or until fragrant. Remove from the heat and add the palm sugar, fish sauce and chilli powder. Allow to cool, then roll into small balls (1 cm/⅓ in diameter). Heat the deep-frying oil in a wok, dip the balls into the batter and deep fry for about 5 minutes, or until golden.

To make the salted fish balls, purée all of the ingredients in a food processor until fine. Roll the mixture into small balls (1 cm/⅓ in diameter). Steam the balls on a flat plate in a steamer for about 10 minutes, or until cooked, then cool. Heat the oil in

1 teaspoon roasted chilli powder
    (see glossary)
1 L (4 cups/1¾ pt) safflower oil for
    deep-frying
Frying batter (see page 25)

SALTED FISH BALLS

1 cup (100 g/4 oz) salted fish,
    grilled and flaked (see glossary)
1 cup (100 g/4 oz) pork, finely
    minced (ground)
1 tablespoon fresh coriander
    (cilantro) leaves
1 tablespoon Chinese shallots
1 teaspoon ground white
    peppercorns
1 L (4 cups/1¾ pt) safflower oil for
    deep-frying
Frying batter (see page 25)

FRIED SALTY RADISH

3 medium dried salted radishes
    (see glossary)
250 g (8 oz) pork fat (back), cut
    into 10 mm x 2.5 mm
    (½ in x ⅛ in) rectangles or
    30 mL (2 tablespoons) safflower
    oil
2 cloves garlic, minced
2 eggs
1 teaspoon castor (superfine) sugar

a wok, dip the balls into the frying batter and deep-fry for about 5 minutes, or until golden.

To make the fried salty radish, wash, dry and shred the radishes (or purchase shredded). Render the fat in a frying pan and when it is beginning to crisp and colour, drain off all but 30 mL (2 tablespoons). (Keep and use the remainder for stir-frying — it is delicious.) Add the garlic and fry for about 3 minutes, or until golden. Add the eggs and sugar, and continue to cook, for about 2–3 minutes, or until the eggs are just set.

DUCK AND EGG NOODLE SOUP WITH CONDIMENTS

Ba Mii Nam Bpet Yang Kreuang Brung

SOUP

1 L (4 cups/1¾ pt) chicken or pork
    stock
30 mL (2 tablespoons) oyster sauce
1 teaspoon palm sugar
1 Chinese roast duck, boned and
    finely sliced (reserve the liquid
    from the cavity)
3 stalks Chinese broccoli or
    3 Chinese cabbage leaves,
    roughly chopped
2 (375 g/12 oz) packets egg noodles
4 cloves garlic, minced and deep-
    fried until golden (see glossary)
½ teaspoon white peppercorns,
    ground
3-4 coriander (cilantro) leaves
3 tablespoons Tsiant preserved
    vegetables (see glossary)

Roasted chilli powder (see glossary)
Chillies with vinegar (see glossary)

SHOULD CHINESE ROAST duck be unobtainable, then duck poached in the stock together with 2 star anise would be more than acceptable. Any Chinese roasted or barbecued meat can be substituted.

Serve this dish with *Kreuang Brung* (condiments) — *Prik Bon* (Roasted Chilli Powder), *Prik Nam Som* (Chillies with Vinegar), *Nam Pla* (fish sauce) which may be infused with chopped chillies (*Nam Pla Prik*) and *Nam Taan Sy* (castor/superfine sugar).

Method: In a large pan bring the stock to the boil, then add the oyster sauce, palm sugar, reserved duck liquid, broccoli or cabbage.

Bring a large pan of salted water to the boil and blanch the egg noodles according to the instructions on the packet. Distribute them evenly between 6 individual bowls. Cover the noodles with the duck slices, then ladle over the stock. Sprinkle with the deep-fried garlic, ground peppercorns, coriander and Tsiant preserved vegetables. Serve with *Kreuang Brung* (the condiments suggested above).

MAIN COURSES

MAIN COURSES

A THAI MEAL IS NOT just a combination of textures and flavours within one dish, but a compilation of all the dishes to be served. There should be no duplication or repetition, but a balance. Not every dish should be served hot, nor should there be too many curries. Complex dishes should be accompanied by simpler ones so that the palate is not overwhelmed or cloyed. This is indicative of the manner in which Thais approach their food: different contrasting flavours, combined with variously textured garnishes that are then blended with rice. It is the compilation of so many small but powerfully flavoured dishes that entertain the palate and avoid tedious repetition.

SALADS

Thai cuisine is a contrast of seasonings: hot, sweet, sour, salty and occasionally bitter flavours combine to achieve *rot chart* where all flavours are in harmony, and none is unintentionally overwhelming. This is nowhere more apparent than in Thai salads, whether one as elusive and delicate as the *Saeng Wa* of Prawns or as robust and searing as a *Larp* from the North-east.

It is of paramount importance to use the best, freshest ingredients available. Use good-quality alternatives rather than second-rate specified ingredients. In Thai salads, the contrasts and interplays of acids and salts would quickly reveal an inferior choice. Having purchased the produce, it is now up to the skill of the cook to treat and season it correctly. This can only be achieved by knowing the individual flavours of the ingredients being used, and the outcome when combining them. Taste the food as it is being assembled and rectify any imbalances before serving.

CURRIES

Curries are the food most associated with Thai cuisine. Originally from southern India, they were cooked in ghee and were heavy with dried spices. The Thais lightened them with the substitution of coconut cream and the addition of fresh spices such as galangal, lemongrass and kaffir lime zest. It is these fresh ingredients that give Thai curries their remarkable character. It is therefore essential to use fresh ingredients wherever possible. Dried or tired ingredients will make for a curry empty in flavour, hollow to taste.

SOUPS

Not relegated to a single course, soups are an integral part of Thai cuisine and are sipped throughout the meal. They range from the subtle and assuaging Omelette Soup to the aggressive and renowned Hot and Sour Soup. Soups counterbalance the dry, sharp flavours of some dishes with their gentleness, or cut the richness of others.

STEAMED DISHES

Steaming is a gentle method of cooking normally reserved for seafood and fish. The water in the steamer should always be boiling before anything is added. Steamed dishes are good with stronger flavoured selections such as *Nam Priks* or hot curries.

STIR-FRIED DISHES

Preparation of Thai food can be intensive, but cooking can be disproportionately short. This is most apparent in stir-fried dishes. Ingredients for a particular dish are selected, assembled and processed, and then are subjected to a fierce heat that cooks them in no more than a few minutes.

DEEP-FRIED DISHES

Thais have two methods of deep-frying. The first is the one with which most Westerners are familiar: items are immersed in hot oil and quickly cooked. In the second, food such as small pieces of pork or whole fish that have been rubbed with salt and marinated in fish sauce are deep-fried in moderately hot oil. The result is crisp, almost brittle food, where texture is of prime importance. Fish or pork treated in this manner is normally served with a *Nam Prik* or *Lon*.

GRILLED DISHES

Thais grill their food over slow-burning charcoal that imparts a wonderful smokiness. Grilled foods are normally accompanied by a dipping sauce, a *Nam Jim*. This is made in a mortar and pestle which is indispensable in the preparation of Thai food. All pastes and sauces are traditionally made in this crucible, some taking longer to produce than others — crushed garlic takes a few seconds while curry pastes can take much, much longer.

RELISHES AND ACCOMPANIMENTS

No meal is considered complete without the inclusion of either a *Nam Prik* or a *Lon*. *Nam Prik* is an ancient Thai dish, probably coming with the Thais as they migrated from the south of China 1000 years ago. *Nam Priks* are always pungent, redolent of roasted kapi (shrimp paste) and hot. They can be as simple as the uncooked Prawn Paste Relish or as complex as Crab and Tamarind. *Lons* are a much gentler food — pork and prawns for example, simmered in coconut cream, then seasoned with tamarind water, palm sugar and fish sauce. These dips or relishes are always eaten with vegetables — raw, blanched or battered and deep-fried — that are normally cut into bite-sized pieces.

Thais enjoy a wide variety of condiments in their cuisine. Pickled or salted, these extremes of flavours help to balance the richness, sweetness or heat of the main dishes. Salty eggs cut the sweetness of a pineapple curry, pickled vegetables balance the richness of a Massaman curry, pickled garlic is a wonderful foil for the heat of a jungle curry. Layer upon layer, contrast and harmony, varying textures — these are the essence of Thai food.

SALADS

CHICKEN AND COCONUT SALAD

Yam Gop Tiam

250 mL (1 cup/8 fl oz) coconut
    cream
30 mL (2 tablespoons) fish sauce
1 tablespoon palm sugar
200 g (7 oz) chicken breast
1 stalk lemongrass, very finely
    sliced
5 red shallots, very finely sliced
    lengthways
4 kaffir lime leaves, finely
    shredded
1 tablespoon fresh coriander
    (cilantro) leaves
1 tablespoon fresh mint leaves, torn
1 fresh large red chilli, deseeded
    and julienned
1 tablespoon roasted peanuts,
    coarsely ground
2 fresh small green chillies, finely
    sliced
1 teaspoon lime juice
1 tablespoon chilli jam (see
    page 85, optional)

THIS SALAD EPITOMISES the Thai approach to salads, in which many strong flavours and textures are combined and tempered by one another. It relies on fresh, prime ingredients, sliced very finely to produce the right texture and flavour. This salad should be very creamy, a little sweet, and salty.

Method: In a medium pan heat the coconut cream with the fish sauce and palm sugar. When the palm sugar has dissolved and the coconut cream is boiling, add the chicken meat and simmer until the meat is cooked (about 10 minutes). Allow the chicken to cool in the cream mixture, then remove the meat and shred it finely. Combine all the remaining ingredients, the shredded chicken and coconut cream mixture, and serve.

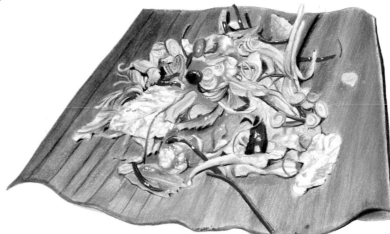

BANANA BLOSSOM SALAD
Yam Hua Plii Sy Gung

1 large banana blossom
45 mL (3 tablespoons) vinegar,
  lime or lemon juice
125 mL (½ cup/4 fl oz) coconut
  cream
2 tablespoons chilli jam (see
  page 85)
15 mL (1 tablespoon) fish sauce (or
  light soy sauce for vegetarians)
1 tablespoon palm sugar
6 medium green prawns (raw
  shrimp), shelled and deveined
  (optional)
1 teaspoon lime juice
2 tablespoons roasted peanuts,
  coarsely ground
2 tablespoons fresh coriander
  (cilantro) leaves

BANANA BLOSSOMS ARE the purple buds that eventually produce a hand of bananas. They are very much like artichokes — they must be peeled and cleaned to their core and then stored in acidulated water. You may substitute chicken for the prawns, or leave them out completely.

Method: Remove the outer sheaths of the banana blossom to reveal the white heart. Quarter the heart, remove the core and stamens (future bananas) and finely slice the quarters on a bias (at a 45 degree angle). Immerse in water, acidulated with vinegar, lime or lemon juice.

In a medium pan bring the coconut cream to the boil, add the chilli jam, fish sauce and palm sugar, and stir until dissolved. Bring to a boil, add the prawns and simmer about 3 minutes or until the prawns are cooked. Add the banana blossom, lime juice and peanuts. Stir to heat through. Transfer the salad to a plate straight away and sprinkle with coriander just before serving.

CRISPY FISH SALAD

Yam Pla Fuu

*200 g (7 oz) flathead, hake or other
    firm, white-fleshed fish, such as
    catfish fillets*
Sea salt
Safflower oil for deep-frying
*½ small, very firm green mango,
    julienned*
*2 tablespoons red shallots, sliced
    lengthways*
4–6 fresh mint leaves, torn
Fresh coriander (cilantro) leaves
*2 tablespoons roasted peanuts,
    coarsely crushed if large*

DRESSING
4–10 fresh small green chillies
Pinch salt
15 mL (1 tablespoon) fish sauce
30 mL (2 tablespoons) lime juice
1 teaspoon castor (superfine) sugar

THIS IS A CLASSIC Thai salad eaten throughout the country, and is especially delicious with a cold beer on a hot day. The secret of its success lies in the contrast of flavours and textures: hot, sour and salty, succulent and crispy.

Method: Wash and dry the fillets, then rub with salt and place them on a rack in a roasting pan, allowing plenty of room between each fillet. Roast the fish in a medium oven (180°C/350°F/Gas mark 4) for 20 minutes or until golden brown. Remove from the pan and allow to cool. Pulse the fish in a food processor with a pinch of salt until it has the consistency of fresh breadcrumbs. Do not over-process as this will affect its ability to puff up.

Half-fill a wok with oil and heat until very hot, almost smoking. Quickly add ½ cup (50 g/2 oz) of the fish and it will puff up into a 'raft'. Using two long-handled spoons or forks, pull the raft of fish towards you. When the oil stops bubbling, turn the raft over and continue to fry until golden brown. Remove and drain on absorbent paper. Repeat with remaining fish.

In a medium bowl, break the fish rafts into large pieces. Add the remaining ingredients and toss gently to combine, transfer to a serving plate. Add the dressing just before serving to ensure that the fish remains crisp.

To make the dressing, crush the chillies with the salt, using a mortar and pestle (or a food processor). Combine with the remaining ingredients.

POMELO SALAD

Yam Som Oo

Pulp from 1 large pomelo
100 g (4 oz) cooked small prawns
    (shrimp), shelled, deveined and
    shredded (optional)
30 g (1 oz) pork, steamed and
    julienned (optional)
3 tablespoons coconut, roasted and
    shredded (see glossary)
2 cloves garlic, sliced lengthways
    and deep-fried (see glossary)
3 red shallots, sliced lengthways
    and deep-fried (see glossary)
1 tablespoon roasted peanuts,
    coarsely ground
2–5 fresh small green chillies,
    finely sliced
4–6 fresh mint leaves, torn
2 tablespoons fresh coriander
    (cilantro) leaves

DRESSING
15 mL (1 tablespoon) fish sauce (or
    light soy sauce for vegetarians)
2 teaspoons palm sugar
1 teaspoon lime juice
1 tablespoon chilli jam (see
    page 85)
30 mL (2 tablespoons) coconut
    cream

A POMELO IS a large succulent citrus fruit. After peeling, segment it, then separate the teardrop-shaped flesh into small fragments. Pomelos are now becoming increasingly available, but should they not be obtainable, mandarins may be used.

Method: Combine all the ingredients, add the dressing and toss well but gently to avoid the pomelo breaking up too much. Serve on a large platter.

To make the dressing, combine all the ingredients: the dressing should taste salty and sweet, not too sour.

Green Mango and Squid Salad

Yam Pla Meuk Mamuang Dip

100 g (4 oz) squid, sliced
1 small, very firm green mango, peeled and julienned
2 tablespoons red shallots, sliced lengthways
1 tablespoon fresh coriander (cilantro) leaves
1 tablespoon fresh mint leaves, torn
3 tablespoons peanuts or cashews, roasted
2 tablespoons red shallots, sliced lengthways and deep-fried (see glossary)
1 clove garlic, sliced and deep-fried (see glossary)

DRESSING
2–5 fresh small green chillies
Pinch salt
1 tablespoon palm sugar
30 mL (2 tablespoons) fish sauce
15 mL (1 tablespoon) lime juice

THIS SALAD RELIES on the sour, crisp succulence of unripened mango, its skin still green, for its success. If one is not available in your supermarket or Asian food store, then have a look in an Indian market. You may find joy (and your mango). Choose a fruit that is hard, shiny and green. Do not use a mango that is half-ripe — better to use a very green apple, dressed in a little lime juice. Prawns or mussels could also be substituted for the squid.

Method: Blanch the squid in boiling salted water for 30 seconds, remove and drain. Combine the squid with the mango, red shallots, coriander, mint and peanuts. Add dressing to the salad, toss well, sprinkle with the deep-fried shallots and garlic, and serve.

To make the dressing, crush the chillies with the salt, using a mortar and pestle (or a food processor), then blend with the remaining ingredients.

GRILLED BANANA CHILLI SALAD

Yam Prik Yuak

10 banana chillies

100 g (4 oz) small cooked prawns (shrimp), shelled and deveined (optional)

15 mL (1 tablespoon) fish sauce (or light soy sauce for vegetarians)

1 teaspoon palm sugar

1 teaspoon lime juice

30 mL (2 tablespoons) coconut cream

2 tablespoons red shallots, sliced lengthways and deep-fried (see glossary)

2 tablespoons fresh coriander (cilantro) leaves

THE SMOKY AND EARTHY flavours of roasted banana chillies make this a wonderful salad. Regular small capsicums (peppers) may be substituted for the banana chillies, and some small prawns may be reserved to sprinkle on top of the salad as a garnish. To make this salad vegetarian, omit the prawns and substitute light soy sauce for the fish sauce.

Method: Grill, broil or roast the whole chillies until charred, then put them into a bowl and cover with plastic wrap to allow the steam to lift the skin. When cool, peel the skin, then tear the chillies into halves or thirds and remove the seeds. It may be necessary to wash the chillies.

Slice the chillies and mix together with the prawns if using. Add the fish sauce, palm sugar and just enough lime juice to sharpen the flavours, not sour them. Mix well.

To serve, transfer to a plate and drizzle with the coconut cream and sprinkle with the shallots and coriander.

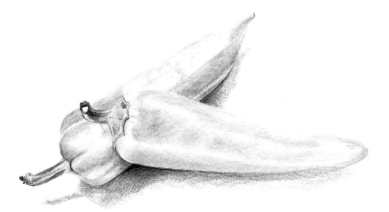

GRILLED LONG EGGPLANT SALAD

Yam Makreua Yaew Pao

4 long green eggplants (aubergines)

2 hardboiled eggs, shelled and quartered

30 g (1 oz) pork, steamed and julienned (optional)

2 tablespoons red shallots, sliced lengthways

15 mL (1 tablespoon) fish sauce (or light soy sauce for vegetarians)

1 teaspoon lime juice

1 teaspoon palm sugar

1 tablespoon fresh coriander (cilantro) leaves

1 tablespoon dried prawns (shrimp), puréed

LONG GREEN EGGPLANTS are available from most Asian food stores, otherwise use a small purple eggplant, which, unlike the Thai eggplant, needs to be salted to remove the bitterness before use. To do this, simply cut it in half lengthways and rub with salt. After no less than 1 hour, wash off the salt and proceed with the recipe.

Omitting the eggs, pork and dried prawns, and substituting light soy sauce for the fish sauce makes a delicious vegetarian salad.

Method: Grill, broil or roast the eggplants until charred and tender, then put them into a bowl and cover with plastic wrap to allow the steam to loosen the skin. When cool, peel and slice the eggplants and arrange on a plate. Garnish with the eggs, pork and shallots.

Just before serving, combine the fish sauce, lime juice and palm sugar in a small bowl and drizzle over the composed salad. Sprinkle with the coriander and ground prawns.

SCALLOP SALAD

Pla Hoi Shenn

150 g (5 oz) scallops
1 stalk lemongrass, very finely
   sliced
2 red shallots, very finely sliced
1 fresh large red chilli, deseeded
   and julienned
2 kaffir lime leaves, finely
   shredded
10–15 fresh mint leaves
10–15 fresh coriander (cilantro)
   leaves
100 g (4 oz) freshly grated coconut
   meat (optional)

DRESSING
1 fresh large red chilli, deseeded
   and chopped
2–4 fresh small green chillies
Pinch salt
1 teaspoon castor (superfine) sugar
15 mL (1 tablespoon) lime juice
15 mL (1 tablespoon) fish sauce

THIS TYPE OF SALAD differs from a *yam* in that the main ingredient is usually only partly cooked and the dressing is saltier. Also, a large amount of lemongrass is used. It needs to be finely sliced into shavings, so that its full flavours can be enjoyed without the fibrous texture.

Method: Blanch the scallops in boiling salted water, then drain. Combine the scallops with the remaining ingredients. To serve, add dressing to the salad and toss well.

To make the dressing, crush the chillies with the salt until fine, using a mortar and pestle (or a food processor), then add the sugar, lime juice and fish sauce. The dressing will taste salty, sour and just a little sweet.

GRILLED BEEF SALAD

Neua Nam Tok

*200 g (7 oz) beef sirloin,
  marinated in a little fish sauce
  for a few hours*
*4 red shallots, finely sliced
  lengthways*
1 tablespoon fresh mint leaves
*1 tablespoon fresh coriander
  (cilantro) leaves*
1 tablespoon Chinese shallot, sliced
*1 tablespoon pak chii farang, sliced
  (see glossary)*
*½–2 teaspoons roasted chilli
  powder (see glossary)*
*2 tablespoons ground roasted sticky
  rice (see glossary)*
30 mL (2 tablespoons) lime juice
*15 mL (1 tablespoon) fish sauce (or
  light soy sauce for vegetarians)*

THIS DISH AND the two following are usually eaten with a side plate of fresh vegetables. Cucumbers, green beans and cabbage make a pleasant combination, but any vegetables may be used as long as they offer an interesting contrast in taste and texture. Pork neck (blade) or some field mushrooms may also be used instead of the beef.

Method: Grill or broil the beef to medium rare, about 3–5 minutes. Allow to rest for at least 5 minutes before slicing thinly. Combine the beef with the remaining ingredients, using 1 tablespoon of sticky rice. Check that the flavour is hot, sour and salty, and add more chillies, lime juice and/or fish sauce as necessary.

Serve sprinkled with the remaining 1 tablespoon of sticky rice.

LARP OF PORK

Larp Muu

200 g (7 oz) pork, minced (ground)
100 g (4 oz) mixed boiled offal such
    as liver, intestine, skin
    (optional)
Pinch salt
15 mL (1 tablespoon) nam pla ra
    (see glossary)
15 mL (1 tablespoon) fish sauce
45 mL (3 tablespoons) lime juice
4 red shallots, sliced lengthways
2 tablespoons fresh mint leaves
2 tablespoons fresh coriander
    (cilantro) leaves
2 tablespoons roasted sticky rice,
    ground (see glossary)
1 tablespoon roasted chilli powder
    (see glossary)

LARP IS A SALAD akin to the primordial steak 'tartare'. This type of *larp* comes from the north-east of Thailand and employs simple cooking techniques to weld together the elemental Thai flavours of hot, salty and sour. *Larp* recalls one of my fondest memories of Thailand, when I was in Nan, a province in the north, during the festival of Songkran. This water festival, celebrated in the middle of April, marks the traditional beginning of the Thai New Year. At the turn of the century, the forehead was anointed with lustral water, symbolically cleansing the previous year's transgressions. One started the year afresh. Now one starts it awash, as the Thais celebrate their New Year with gusto. On Songkran and the following few days, the Thais' typical reticence and reserve is forgotten as, with abandon, they lustily anoint anybody or anything with buckets of water. Nobody is safe. In Nan, they celebrate with special fervour — overlooking a shallow river, I was eating some *Larp Muu*, having a beer and chuckling while I watched the city fire truck in the middle of the river, spraying all, honouring their New Year.

Method: In a medium pan simmer the pork (and the offal if using) in a little salted water for 3 minutes or until cooked.

Just before serving, stir in the *nam pla ra*, fish sauce and lime juice, then the remaining ingredients. Check that the flavour is hot, salty and sour. Add a few extra drops of lime juice to sharpen and define the flavours if necessary.

LARP OF CHIANG MAI
Larp Chiang Mai

30 mL (2 tablespoons) safflower oil

2 cloves garlic, crushed

100 g (4 oz) beef, minced (ground), not too lean

100 g (4 oz) assorted offal (optional)

1 tablespoon fish sauce

2 tablespoons chicken stock

2 tablespoons Chinese shallots, chopped

2 tablespoons red shallots, sliced lengthways

2 tablespoons fresh coriander (cilantro) leaves

2 tablespoons fresh Vietnamese mint leaves, shredded

LARP PASTE

4 red shallots

3 cloves garlic

2-6 dried large red chillies, deseeded and grilled (broiled)

1 stalk lemongrass, finely sliced

1 tablespoon galangal, shredded and roasted

10 white peppercorns

½ teaspoon mace, ground and roasted

4 cloves, roasted and ground

1 teaspoon salt

1 teaspoon kapi (shrimp paste), roasted (see glossary)

IT IS ONLY since the 1920s that the north of Thailand has become accessible — before the opening of a railroad, it often took several weeks of arduous journey, on elephant or by boat, before reaching the northern capital, Chiang Mai. This isolation from the central plains, the heartland of Thai culture, meant that northern architecture, language and many other aspects of life evolved differently. Northern food, for example, is not as hot, nor does it use coconut cream in curries. The food is more robust and less complicated in taste and technique. This *larp* (salad) is very fragrant and should be eaten with fresh vegetables such as cabbage, green beans and cucumbers. Chicken, duck or pork can easily replace the beef.

Method: Heat the oil in a pan and fry the garlic until golden. Add the *larp* paste and continue to fry for a few minutes until fragrant. Add the meat and the offal (if using) and moisten with the fish sauce and stock. Simmer for 3 minutes or until cooked.

To serve, add the two types of shallot, coriander and mint to the meat. The *larp* will taste salty and be fragrant from the fresh and dried spices.

To make the *larp* paste, roast the shallots and garlic in a wok until charred, then peel. Purée all of the ingredients in a food processor using as little water as possible.

SAENG WA OF GRILLED PRAWNS

Saeng Wa Gung Pao

6 medium prawns (shrimp), grilled
    or broiled in their shells, peeled
    and finely shredded
6 red shallots, finely sliced
    lengthways
1 stalk lemongrass, finely sliced
5 kaffir lime leaves, finely sliced
3 tablespoons young ginger,
    julienned
½ fresh long red chilli, deseeded
    and julienned
2 tablespoons fresh coriander
    (cilantro) leaves
1 tablespoon fresh mint leaves

DRESSING
2 tablespoons palm sugar
30 mL (2 tablespoons) fish sauce
30 mL (2 tablespoons) lime juice
Juice of 1 fresh kaffir lime or
    15 mL (1 tablespoon) thick
    tamarind water (see glossary)

TYPICAL OF ROYAL THAI food, this salad uses finely honed techniques and unusual combinations of flavours and textures to revive jaded palates. Kaffir lime juice is rarely used in Thai cookery — in fact normally the juice is used to rinse the hair, removing, the Thais believe, any malevolent influence that might be lurking. Hardly culinary! Kaffir lime juice has a wonderfully pervasive perfume, which is the essence of this dressing, adding a further dimension of flavour through fragrance. Only juice from the fresh kaffir lime can be used for this, as that of the frozen fruit is somewhat bitter and cloying. If fresh kaffir lime juice is unavailable, use thick tamarind water, perhaps perfumed with a little mandarin juice. If large, the prawns should be deveined and grilled in their shells, giving them greater flavour, then shredded. Small prawns can also be used. Every ingredient in this salad is shredded in order to allow, in one spoonful, the composite taste of the whole. Rather than one overpowering another, all flavours sparkle in that one spoonful. This is the quintessence of good Thai food. Ideally, this dish should be served with sweet pork, crispy fish and a plate of fresh vegetables, such as sliced cucumbers, Thai basil and green beans.

Method: Combine all of the ingredients, add the dressing, toss the salad, and serve.

To make the dressing, dissolve the palm sugar in the fish sauce. Combine all the ingredients — the desired flavour is sour, salty and sweet.

CURRIES

ROAST DUCK CURRY

Gaeng Pet Bet Yang

250 mL (1 cup/8 fl oz) coconut
    cream
3 tablespoons of the curry paste
30 mL (2 tablespoons) fish sauce
1 tablespoon palm sugar
325 mL (1½ cups/12 fl oz) coconut
    milk
½ Chinese roast duck, boned and
    neatly sliced, together with the
    liquid from the duck's cavity
2 fresh long red chillies, halved
    and deseeded
4 kaffir lime leaves, torn
2 apple eggplants (aubergines),
    quartered and finely sliced
50 g (2 oz) pea eggplants (aubergines)
20-25 fresh Thai basil leaves

CURRY PASTE
6-10 dried red chillies, deseeded
    and chopped
4 red shallots, chopped
6 cloves garlic, chopped
1 stalk lemongrass, finely sliced
½ tablespoon chopped galangal
1 tablespoon coriander (cilantro)
    root, scraped and chopped
½ tablespoon kaffir lime zest
1 teaspoon white peppercorns
1 teaspoon coriander (cilantro)
    seeds, roasted
½ teaspoon cumin seeds, roasted
3 cloves, roasted
3 blades mace, roasted
1 teaspoon salt
1 teaspoon kapi (shrimp paste),
    roasted (see glossary)

THIS CURRY FROM Bangkok shows how readily the Thais adapt new and foreign ingredients. Originally it would have been made with a fresh duck, cut into small pieces. As more Chinese settled in Bangkok, the Thais made use of their red roasting techniques, amongst other things, and used the roast duck that is available in the Chinatown of every major city. At the turn of this century pineapple, tomatoes and even grapes were used instead of the eggplants to garnish this curry.

Method: In a medium pan, boil the coconut cream over medium heat for 3–5 minutes or until it has separated, stirring constantly to ensure that the cream does not scorch. Add the curry paste, stirring constantly to prevent the paste from burning. Fry for 5 minutes or until the colour of the paste deepens and it smells fragrant. Add the fish sauce and palm sugar and continue frying for a further 1–2 minutes. The paste should be marbled with coconut oil, almost clotting. Then add the coconut milk and bring to the boil. Add the remaining ingredients and simmer for a few moments, allowing the flavours to combine and ripen. This curry is slightly salty, sweet and creamy. Serve with garnish vegetables.

To make the curry paste, purée the chillies with the fresh ingredients in a food processor until very fine. Grind all the spices and combine with the purée.

Note: The amount of pea eggplants used can vary as these are an acquired taste.

CHICKEN CURRY WITH GINGER

Gaeng Sap Nok King Orn

250 mL (1 cup/8 fl oz) coconut
   cream, a little more if necessary
3 tablespoons julienned ginger
2 tablespoons of the curry paste
1 tablespoon palm sugar
45 mL (3 tablespoons) fish sauce
200 g (7 oz) chicken, preferably
   thighs, minced (ground)
325 mL (1½ cups/12 fl oz) coconut
   milk
1 fresh long red chilli, cut in half,
   deseeded and julienned
4-6 kaffir lime leaves, shredded
1 apple eggplant (aubergine),
   destemmed, quartered and
   finely sliced
10 pea eggplants (aubergines)
   (optional)
50 g (2 oz) snake (long green)
   beans, cut into 2 cm (¾ in)
   lengths
10-12 Thai basil leaves

CURRY PASTE
4-8 dried large red chillies,
   deseeded
1 stalk lemongrass, finely sliced
1 teaspoon galangal, peeled and
   finely sliced
4 cloves garlic, chopped
4 red shallots, sliced
1 tablespoon coriander (cilantro) roots
1 teaspoon kaffir lime zest
1 teaspoon kapi (shrimp paste),
   roasted (see glossary)
1 teaspoon salt
10 white peppercorns, ground

KHUN CHARLIE AMATYAKUL, a well-known Thai chef and gourmand, first introduced this curry to me. It is an elegant dish relying on fine knife work and prime ingredients. The ginger must be fresh and new-season white ginger (available mid-late summer). If such young ginger is unobtainable, then mature ginger can be used. The julienne should be washed in salted water to reduce its pungency. Any poultry may be used. In fact, the Thais often replace the chicken with freshwater fish in this style of curry — either minced, ground or puréed and formed into balls — often substituting krachai for the ginger and omitting the eggplants.

Method: In a medium pan, boil the coconut cream over medium heat, stirring constantly until it separates, 3-5 minutes. Add 1 tablespoon of the ginger and all the curry paste and fry for about 5 minutes until the paste is fragrant, quite red in colour and marbled with the coconut oil; add more cream if the paste is too dry. Add 1 more tablespoon of ginger and the palm sugar, and continue to fry for about 2 minutes or until the colour further deepens. Stir in the fish sauce and the final tablespoon of ginger, then add the chicken. Fry until the meat is cooked, 3-5 minutes, stirring constantly to prevent it from clumping together. Add the coconut milk, bring to a boil and then stir in the remaining ingredients. Check the flavour: it should be salty, sweet and fragrant from the ginger and basil. Rest for a minute or two before serving to allow the flavours to ripen. Reheat slightly.

To make the curry paste, purée all the ingredients in a food processor, with as little water as possible, until fine.

LIGHT RED CURRY OF BEANCURD

Chuu Chii Tor Huu

*250 mL (1 cup/8 fl oz) coconut
   cream*
2 tablespoons of the curry paste
15 mL (1 tablespoon) fish sauce
1 teaspoon palm sugar
*150 g (5 oz) soft white beancurd
   (tofu), rinsed*
*125 mL (½ cup/4 fl oz) coconut
   milk, approximately*
*1 long red fresh chilli, cut in half,
   deseeded and julienned*
*5 kaffir lime leaves, finely
   shredded*
*2 tablespoons coriander (cilantro)
   leaves*

CURRY PASTE
*3-5 dried long red chillies,
   deseeded and chopped*
4 red shallots, sliced
2 cloves garlic, sliced
½ stalk lemongrass, sliced
1 teaspoon galangal, chopped
½ teaspoon kaffir lime zest
1 teaspoon coriander (cilantro) root
1 teaspoon salt
*1 teaspoon kapi (shrimp paste),
   roasted (see glossary)*
10 white peppercorns, ground

THIS RED CURRY sauce can be used with any vegetable or seafood, not just beancurd. Some field mushrooms or green beans, for example, are equally delicious. *Chuu Chii* is an onomatopoeia for the sound of the curry frying in the coconut cream. Sometimes, the coconut milk that is used to moisten this curry is omitted.

Method: In a medium pan boil the coconut cream over high heat until the cream has separated, about 5 minutes, then add the curry paste and fry for a few minutes until it is fragrant. Add the fish sauce and palm sugar and continue to fry until the colour deepens. Add the beancurd and moisten with the coconut milk to prevent the paste from catching. When the beancurd is heated through (about 3-4 minutes) check that the curry is salty and a little oily, then carefully mix in the chilli and the kaffir lime leaves, as the beancurd is very delicate and breaks up easily.

To serve, sprinkle with the coriander.

To make the curry paste, purée all the ingredients in a food processor, using as little water as possible.

THICK RED CURRY OF BEEF
Panaeng Neua

*500 mL (2 cups/16 fl oz) coconut
  cream*
4 tablespoons of the curry paste
45 mL (3 tablespoons) fish sauce
3 tablespoons palm sugar
*250 mL (1 cup/8 fl oz) coconut
  milk*
*200 g (7 oz) beef rump (sirloin),
  finely sliced*
*2 fresh large red chillies, roll cut
  (see glossary)*
4 kaffir lime leaves, torn
20-30 fresh Thai basil leaves

CURRY PASTE
*5 dried long red chillies, deseeded
  and chopped*
6 cloves garlic, chopped
4 red shallots, sliced
1 stalk lemongrass, finely sliced
*½ tablespoon galangal, peeled and
  chopped*
*1 tablespoon coriander (cilantro)
  roots*
½ tablespoon kaffir lime zest
½ teaspoon white peppercorns
*1 teaspoon coriander (cilantro)
  seeds, roasted*
½ teaspoon cumin seeds, roasted
1 crushed nutmeg, roasted
Pinch salt
*1 teaspoon kapi (shrimp paste),
  roasted (see glossary)*
*2 tablespoons peanuts, roasted and
  ground*

A RELATION OF THE rendang curries of Malaysia and
Indonesia, this curry is a favourite of all Thais. It is
not too hot, and is rich and creamy from the coconut
cream and peanuts. Thais normally do not like to eat
beef, but this curry is the exception. Chicken or pork
can be substituted.

Method: In a medium pan, boil the coconut cream
over a high heat, stirring constantly to prevent the
cream from scorching, until it has separated, about
8–10 minutes. Add the curry paste and fry, stirring
constantly for about 10 minutes or until the paste is
fragrant. Add the fish sauce and the palm sugar and
continue to fry until the colour deepens. Moisten
with the coconut milk and simmer until the milk has
almost evaporated. Then add the beef and simmer
until the meat is cooked as desired, 1–2 minutes for
medium rare. Garnish with the chillies, kaffir lime
leaves and basil leaves, and serve. The flavour should
be salty, sweet and creamy. Add more fish sauce and/
or palm sugar if needed.

To make the curry paste, in a food processor purée
the chillies with the fresh ingredients in as little
water as possible. Grind all the spices and combine
with the purée, then add the peanuts.

GREEN CURRY OF PORK

Gaeng Gwiow Wan Muu

250 mL (1 cup/8 fl oz) coconut cream

500 mL (2 cups/16 fl oz) coconut milk

1 teaspoon salt

200 g (7 oz) pork spareribs (or any other braising cut of pork), cut into 5 cm (2 in) lengths

4 kaffir lime leaves, torn into quarters, and their stalks

2 tablespoons of the curry paste

30 mL (2 tablespoons) fish sauce

3-4 fresh small green chillies, crushed

2 fresh long red chillies, deseeded and cut on a bias

10-12 fresh Thai basil leaves

3 stalks krachai, peeled and shredded (see glossary, optional)

100 g (4 oz) pea eggplants (aubergines)

CURRY PASTE

1-2 tablespoons fresh small green chillies, chopped

2 fresh long green chillies, deseeded and chopped

6 red shallots, chopped

3 cloves garlic, chopped

1 stalk lemongrass, finely chopped

1 tablespoon galangal, peeled and finely sliced

1 tablespoon coriander (cilantro) root

2 teaspoons kaffir lime zest

5 white peppercorns

KHUN YAI (SOMBAT JANPHETCHARA) was the first person to teach me how to cook Thai food. When I tasted her cooking I realised that Thai food is one of the world's greatest cuisines — the clarity of flavours, the definition of textures, all combine to make a singularly sophisticated food. Khun Yai learnt her art from her mother, who was attached to the Thai court. For several months I went to learn her subtle wielding of flavours. This curry is her recipe. It is a versatile curry in that, like the rest of Thai food, quantities are variable. When the Thais cook they cook by taste, not by recipes alone. They use recipes as guidelines to be followed and fine-tuned by the cook. In some of the older recipe books there are often ingredients listed but no quantities are given — recipes were used as an aide memoire, to assist the cook in the cooking. One recipe calls for a mother's knuckle of ginger! Khun Yai cooks in the old way, rarely following recipes, recalling and measuring by volume the required quantities, unable to describe or break down a recipe except by the doing. Obscure though her practice was, her cooking was and is still sublime.

Method: In a medium saucepan bring to the boil the combined coconut cream and milk and salt. Add the pork and kaffir lime stalks (the leaves are for garnishing) and simmer for about 20 minutes or until the pork is tender. Skim occasionally during cooking and reserve the foam that forms on the top of the coconut milk. When the meat is tender, boil the foam residue in another pan until it has separated. Add the curry paste and fry over a medium heat, stirring constantly, for 3-4 minutes or until it is fragrant. Add the fish sauce and fry for another minute.

½ teaspoon coriander (cilantro)
seeds, roasted
¼ teaspoon cumin seeds, roasted
2-3 blades mace, roasted
1 teaspoon kapi (shrimp paste),
roasted (see glossary)
1 teaspoon salt

Combine the pork with the milk and cream mixture. Add the chillies, basil, kaffir lime leaves, krachai (if using) and eggplants and simmer for a few moments. Remove from heat and serve immediately.

To make the curry paste, purée all the fresh ingredients in a food processor, using as little water as possible, until fine. Grind all the dried spices, mix in the salt and combine with the purée.

PINEAPPLE CURRY OF MUSSELS

Gaeng Sapparot Hoi Malaeng Puu

250 mL (1 cup/8 fl oz) coconut
   cream
2 tablespoons of the curry paste
30 mL (2 tablespoons) fish sauce
1 tablespoon palm sugar
15 mL (1 tablespoon) thick
   tamarind water (see glossary)
500 mL (2 cups/16 fl oz) coconut
   milk
500 g (1 lb) mussels, cleaned
½ medium pineapple, peeled and
   chopped
3-4 kaffir lime leaves, torn
2 fresh large red chillies, cut in
   half and deseeded

CURRY PASTE
3-5 dried large red chillies,
   deseeded and chopped
1 stalk lemongrass, finely sliced
1 tablespoon galangal, peeled and
   sliced
4 red shallots, sliced
3 cloves garlic, chopped
1 teaspoon kaffir lime zest
1 teaspoon white peppercorns,
   ground
2 tablespoons roasted fish
   (smoked trout is a
   good alternative)
1 teaspoon kapi (shrimp paste),
   roasted (see glossary)
1 teaspoon salt

PINEAPPLE CURRIES ARE wonderfully delicious. Traditionally Thais use the eggs from a horseshoe crab to complement the fruit. I find the less arcane mussel is a more than satisfactory alternative. Mud crab, large prawns (shrimp), chicken or pork can also be used. Although the combination of meat or seafood with pineapple may for some be hackneyed, in this instance at least, do not dismiss it. An appropriate, if somewhat unusual, side dish is *Kai Kem* (Salty Eggs, see page 116).

Method: In a medium pan, boil and separate the coconut cream over a medium heat, stirring constantly to prevent the cream scorching. Add the curry paste and fry, stirring constantly, for about 4 minutes or until the paste is fragrant. Add the fish sauce, palm sugar and tamarind water, and continue frying for a few moments until the colour deepens and the sugar cooks. Pour in the coconut milk and when the curry comes to the boil, add the mussels, pineapple and kaffir lime leaves. Turn down the heat and simmer until the mussels open, 3-7 minutes.

Just before serving, stir in the chillies and check that the flavour is salty, sweet and sour, adjusting, if necessary, with either some more fish sauce, tamarind water or palm sugar.

To make the curry paste, purée all the ingredients in a food processor, using as little water as possible, until fine.

JUNGLE CURRY OF GUINEA FOWL
Gaeng Ba Gai Dor

15 mL (1 tablespoon) safflower oil

1 tablespoon of the curry paste

15 mL (1 tablespoon) fish sauce

100 g (4 oz) guinea fowl meat,
  finely sliced

300 mL (½ pt) chicken stock

1 tablespoon Mekhong whisky

2 tablespoons pea eggplants
  (aubergines)

50 g (2 oz) snake (long green) beans,
  cut into 2 cm (1 in) lengths

50 g (2 oz) bamboo shoots,
  shredded

10-12 fresh holy basil leaves

4 krachai stalks, scraped and
  julienned (see glossary)

1 tablespoon fresh green
  peppercorns

3 kaffir lime leaves, torn

CURRY PASTE

1½ tablespoons small fresh green
  chillies, chopped

4 red shallots, chopped

4 cloves garlic, chopped

1 stalk lemongrass, finely sliced

1 tablespoon galangal, peeled and
  finely sliced

2 small coriander (cilantro) roots,
  sliced

½ tablespoon kaffir lime zest

3 krachai roots, peeled and sliced

10 white peppercorns, ground

1 tablespoon kapi (shrimp
  paste), roasted (see
  glossary)

1 teaspoon salt

IT WAS AT the beautiful ruins of Sukothai during the festival of Loy Krathong that I had my first jungle curry. Sukothai, on the northern central plains, is considered to be the first truly Thai kingdom. It flourished from the mid thirteenth to the early fifteenth century and was the birthplace of the charming Loy Krathong festival, in which, under a bright moon, people go to their nearest river or klong and there launch candlelit rafts, usually made from banana leaves, to celebrate the successful planting of the next rice crop. That first jungle curry was of wild boar and bamboo. Of less exotic ingredients is the following recipe. Game, any meat or freshwater fish may be used.

Method: In a medium pan, heat the oil over medium-high heat, add the curry paste and fry, stirring constantly, for a few minutes until the paste is fragrant. Add the fish sauce and continue to fry for another minute. Add the meat and continue cooking until the meat is sealed. Cover with the stock and add the Mekhong whisky. Simmer for 1–2 minutes until the meat is cooked but not toughened.

Just before serving, add the remaining ingredients and simmer for a few minutes to cook and allow the flavours to ripen. The flavour should be salty and hot — perhaps a little extra fish sauce may be necessary.

To make the curry paste, purée all the ingredients in a food processor, using as little water as possible, until fine.

MASSAMAN CURRY

Gaeng Mussaman

750 mL (3 cups/1¼ pt) coconut
    milk
Pinch salt
1 L (4 cups/1¾ pt) coconut cream
300 g (10 oz) good braising beef
    such as shin or brisket, cut into
    2 cm (¾ in) cubes and
    deep-fried until brown
2 cm (¾ in) length cassia bark,
    grilled, broiled or roasted
6 bay leaves, roasted
4 cardamom pods, roasted
5 medium potatoes, peeled,
    quartered and deep-fried
15 pickling onions, peeled and
    deep-fried
4 tablespoons peanuts, roasted
All of the curry paste
45 mL (3 tablespoons) fish sauce
3-4 tablespoons palm sugar
45 mL (3 tablespoons) thick
    tamarind water (see glossary)

CURRY PASTE
6-10 large dried red chillies,
    deseeded, chopped and roasted
6 red shallots, roasted (see glossary)
6 cloves garlic, roasted (see
    glossary)
1 teaspoon sliced galangal, roasted
    (see glossary)
½ stalk lemongrass, sliced and
    roasted
2 tablespoons coriander (cilantro)
    roots, chopped
½ teaspoon kaffir lime zest

THIS CURRY ORIGINALLY came from Persia, probably arriving with Muslim courtiers who were attached to the Siamese court. The Thais are very confident of the strength and versatility of their culture, hence they adapt new and foreign influences without reluctance and with great talent, making them peculiarly their own. This 'siamesing' is especially reflected in their food. Before the Portuguese arrived in the mid seventeenth century, the Thais did not know of chillies, yet today Thai food would be unimaginable without them. This curry, once the food of foreigners, is now one of the most popular with the Thais. Appropriate accompaniments might include steamed or deep-fried Salty Eggs (see page 116) or Stuffed Banana Chillies (see page 24). To make this a vegetarian dish, omit the beef, increase the amount of potatoes and substitute light soy sauce for the fish sauce.

Method: In a medium pan bring to a boil the coconut milk, salt and 250 mL (1 cup/8 fl oz) of the coconut cream. Add the beef, cassia bark, bay leaves and cardamom pods, and simmer for 30–40 minutes or until the beef is tender.

Add the potatoes, onions and peanuts, and simmer until the potatoes are cooked — this should only take a few minutes if the vegetables have been sufficiently deep-fried.

In a separate, smaller pan, boil the remaining coconut cream until it separates. Add the curry paste and fry over medium heat for 10 minutes, stirring constantly, until it is fragrant and oily and has quite a deep colour. You may need to moisten the paste occasionally with some of the beef braising liquid.

15 white peppercorns
1 tablespoon coriander (cilantro)
  seeds, roasted
½ tablespoon cumin seeds, roasted
½ nutmeg, crushed and roasted
4 blades mace, roasted
2 cm (¾ in) length cassia bark,
  grilled, broiled or roasted
5 cloves, roasted
5 Thai cardamom pods, roasted ·
1 teaspoon salt

Do not allow the paste to scorch or the curry will have an acrid taste. When the paste is deep mahogany in colour, add the fish sauce and palm sugar and continue cooking for 2–3 minutes. Stir in the tamarind water and then combine with the beef mixture. Simmer for 5 minutes to allow the flavours to combine, then check that it tastes sweet, salty and slightly sour. Adjust, if necessary with either more fish sauce, palm sugar or tamarind water.

To make the curry paste, purée the chillies with the fresh ingredients in a food processor, using as little water as possible, until fine. Grind all the dried spices, mix in the salt and combine with the purée.

INDIAN-STYLE CURRY
Gaeng Kari Pla

250 mL (1 cup/8 fl oz) coconut
    cream
2 tablespoons of the curry paste
1 teaspoon palm sugar
45 mL (3 tablespoons) fish sauce
500 mL (2 cups/16 fl oz) coconut
    milk
3 medium potatoes, peeled,
    quartered and blanched in
    salted water
4 kingfish cutlets or any well-
    flavoured and textured fish,
    such as hake, amberjack or
    mahi-mahi

CURRY PASTE
7 large dried red chillies, deseeded
    and chopped
6 red shallots, chopped
4 cloves garlic, chopped
1 teaspoon galangal, peeled and
    sliced
1 stalk lemongrass, sliced
10 white peppercorns, ground
½ coriander (cilantro) root
1 teaspoon coriander (cilantro)
    seeds, roasted
½ teaspoon cumin seeds, roasted
1 nutmeg, crushed and roasted
3 cardamom pods, roasted
2 tablespoons curry powder
½ teaspoon salt

LIKE THE PREVIOUS recipe, this curry employs a lot of dried spices. This usually indicates a curry of foreign origin, since the Thais are quite sparing in their use of dried spices. They consider that when used in excess, they distort or mask *rot chart* (balance of flavours). The spices that they normally use in curries are coriander (cilantro) seed, cumin seed and white peppercorns. This curry is always accompanied by a relish — the Cucumber Relish on page 14 is a particularly good one. A vegetarian alternative would be to substitute pumpkin for the fish and light soy sauce for the fish sauce.

Method: In a medium pot, over medium heat, boil the coconut cream until it separates, about 3 minutes. Add the curry paste and fry, stirring constantly, for several minutes until fragrant. Add the palm sugar and fish sauce. Continue cooking for a further few minutes then add the coconut milk and bring to a boil, then add the potatoes and simmer for 10 minutes or until they are almost cooked. Add the fish and check the flavour when cooked, 3–5 minutes. It will taste rich and salty, and fragrant from the spices. Add more fish sauce and/or palm sugar if needed. Serve with cucumber relish.

To make the curry paste, purée the chillies with the fresh ingredients in a food processor, using as little water as possible, until fine. Grind all the spices, mix in the salt and combine with the purée.

BURMESE-STYLE PORK CURRY

Gaeng Hang Lae

60 mL (4 tablespoons) safflower oil
All of the curry paste
300 g (10 oz) pork belly, fresh
    bacon or pork leg with the skin
    attached, cut into 2 cm (¾ in)
    cubes
200 g (7 oz) pork neck (blade), cut
    into 2 cm (¾ in) cubes
30 mL (2 tablespoons) thick soy
    sauce or fish sauce
30 mL (2 tablespoons) thick
    tamarind water (see glossary)
1 teaspoon palm sugar
1 cup (4 oz) ginger, julienned
5 heads pickled garlic (see page
    118), cut in half and the outer
    skin peeled, together with
    their juice
10 red shallots, chopped

CURRY PASTE
4 dried long red chillies, deseeded
    and chopped
5 red shallots, chopped
5 cloves garlic, chopped
½ stalk lemongrass, finely sliced
1 teaspoon kapi (shrimp paste),
    roasted (see glossary)
2 tablespoons Gaeng Hang Lae
    powder or 1 tablespoon curry
    powder (see glossary), 2 star
    anise, roasted and 2 cm (¾ in)
    length cassia bark, roasted
1 teaspoon salt

FOR A PERIOD of 200 years Chiang Mai was under the sovereignty of Burma. And it is from that country that this curry originally came, but the Thais adapted it and now it is standard Chiang Mai fare. I got this recipe from Khun Wipat Burupat — or, as she is affectionately called, Bpa (Aunty) Pen — one of the few people who still cook northern food authentically.

Method: In a medium pan, heat the oil, add the curry paste and fry for 5 minutes until fragrant. Add the pork and fry for a further 5 minutes, turning the meat constantly. Add the soy or fish sauce, tamarind water and palm sugar, then add the ginger, garlic and its juice and shallots. Cover with water and simmer for 30 minutes, or until the pork is tender. When the pork is cooked, check that the flavours are salty, sweet and a little sour. Add soy or fish sauce, tamarind water and/or palm sugar, if necessary. The curry should be quite thick. It improves in the keeping and will last for up to 10 days. When reheating add a little extra water. Serve with fresh vegetables.

To make the curry paste, purée the chillies with the fresh ingredients in a food processor, using as little water as possible, until fine. Grind all the dried spices, mix in the salt and combine with the purée.

SOUR ORANGE CURRY WITH SNAKE BEANS

Gaeng Som Pla Tua Fak Yaew

300 mL (½ pt) chicken stock
Pinch salt
1 teaspoon sugar
45-75 mL (3-5 tablespoons) thick
tamarind water (see glossary)
2 tablespoons of the curry paste
200 g (7 oz) snake (long green)
beans, cut into 2.5 cm (1 in)
lengths
2-3 leaves Chinese cabbage,
coarsely cut
1 large river trout or freshwater
fish, filleted or in cutlets
30 mL (2 tablespoons) fish sauce

CURRY PASTE
6-12 dried long red chillies,
deseeded and chopped
6 red shallots, chopped
3 cloves garlic, chopped
1 teaspoon galangal, peeled and
chopped
1 teaspoon salt
1 teaspoon kapi (shrimp paste),
roasted (see glossary)
2 tablespoons ground dried prawns
(shrimp)

PRIMITIVE BUT DELICIOUS, this curry requires only a few ingredients and very little technique, but the results are delicious. Freshwater fish is best for this dish, but any type of seafood will do. Any vegetable can be used as well if a vegetarian dish is desired. The fish or vegetable is used to thicken the curry and to add texture. In Thailand this curry would be served in a metal fish-shaped bowl, over some hot coals. An omelette or steamed eggs would be a good accompaniment.

Method: In a medium pan, combine the stock, salt, sugar and 15 mL (1 tablespoon) of the tamarind water. Bring to a boil. Return the stock to a boil and stir in the curry paste and the vegetables; simmer for 2-3 minutes, or until the vegetables are cooked. Add the fish and continue simmering for 3-5 minutes, or until the fish is cooked.

Just before serving, add the fish sauce and remaining tamarind water. It should taste hot, sour and salty. Add more fish sauce and/or tamarind water as needed.

To make the curry paste, purée all of the ingredients in a food processor, using as little water as possible, until fine.

YELLOW CURRY

Gaeng Leuang

300 mL (½ pt) chicken stock
2 tablespoons of the curry paste
30 mL (2 tablespoons) thick
    tamarind water (see glossary)
1 teaspoon white (granulated)
    sugar
25 mL (1½ tablespoons) fish sauce
1 small green pawpaw (papaya),
    peeled, quartered, deseeded and
    finely sliced or *substitute unripe*
    pineapple, pickled or *fresh*
    bamboo, or *green mango*
250 g (8 oz) snapper, or *any firm,*
    white-fleshed fish fillet, cubed
Juice of 1 lime (optional)

CURRY PASTE
5 orange chillies, chopped
    (optional)
8-16 dried small red chillies,
    chopped
5 cloves garlic, chopped
3 red shallots, chopped
1 stalk lemongrass, sliced
1 tablespoon fresh turmeric
1 tablespoon kapi (shrimp paste),
    raw
1 teaspoon salt

THIS IS A SOUTHERN version of a sour orange curry. Southern food is distinguished by its heat — instead of using dried long red chillies, the small ones are preferred. The use of kapi, usually unroasted in this recipe, gives a rich taste to the finished curry. If a vegetarian curry is required, substitute cauliflower, green beans, tomatoes or cucumbers for the fish, and light soy sauce for the fish sauce.

Method: In a medium pan, bring the stock to the boil and add the curry paste. Return to the boil, then add the tamarind water, sugar and half the fish sauce. Add the pawpaw and boil for about 3–4 minutes, or until the flesh is tender. Add the fish and continue to simmer for 5 minutes or until the fish is cooked.

Just before serving, check the seasoning: sour, salty and very hot is the desired flavour. Adjust with the reserved fish sauce and lime juice (if desired).

To make the curry paste, purée all of the ingredients in a food processor, using as little water as possible, until fine.

STEAMED CURRY

Hor Mawk Pla

300 g (10 oz) firm-fleshed fish
    (such as red fish or orange
    roughy), finely sliced
500 mL (2 cups/16 fl oz) coconut
    cream
15 mL (1 tablespoon) fish sauce
1 teaspoon castor (superfine) sugar
3 tablespoons of the curry paste
1 egg
6 kaffir lime leaves, shredded,
    reserving a little to garnish
10-12 fresh Thai basil leaves
½ long fresh red chilli, deseeded
    and julienned

CURRY PASTE
1 teaspoon krachai (see glossary,
    optional)
10-15 large dried red chillies,
    deseeded and chopped
1 stalk lemongrass, sliced
1 tablespoon galangal, peeled and
    shredded
5 red shallots, chopped
4 cloves garlic
½ tablespoon coriander (cilantro)
    root
1 teaspoon kaffir lime zest
    (optional)
1 teaspoon kapi (shrimp paste),
    roasted (see glossary)
1 teaspoon salt

TRADITIONALLY, THIS CURRY is steamed in a banana leaf cup. Do not steam over too high a heat as this will cause the curry to separate. For a delicious vegetarian alternative, use mushrooms or corn instead of the fish.

Method: Place the fish in a medium bowl and gradually incorporate the coconut cream into the fish, reserving 15 mL (1 tablespoon) for garnish — the cream must not curdle. Mix in the fish sauce, sugar, curry paste, egg and kaffir lime leaves. Line a deep heatproof bowl with the basil leaves, then fill with the mixture. Steam over a medium heat for about 20 minutes or until cooked. Test by inserting a wooden skewer into the mixture — if it comes out clean, it is cooked. Serve drizzled with the reserved coconut cream, and sprinkle with the reserved kaffir lime leaves and the chilli.

To make the curry paste, purée all of the ingredients in a food processor using as little water as possible.

HOT AND SOUR SOUP OF WHITE FISH

Tom Yam Pla

500 mL (2 cups/16 fl oz) chicken
   stock
Pinch salt
2 stalks lemongrass
5 slices galangal
3-4 red shallots
2 coriander (cilantro) roots
1 medium (350 g/11 oz) whiting or
   cod, gutted, scaled and sliced
6 straw or oyster mushrooms
4 kaffir lime leaves, torn
30 mL (2 tablespoons) fish sauce
Pinch sugar (optional, to taste)
5-10 small fresh green chillies,
   pounded
45 mL (3 tablespoons) lime juice
2 tablespoons fresh coriander
   (cilantro) leaves

ALTHOUGH TO THE Westerner *Tom Yam* is synonymous with prawns, to the Thais it is a whole range of soups that are hot and sour — to what degree is determined by individual preference and the ingredients being used. It is an uncomplicated soup therefore it becomes even more important to use prime, fresh ingredients. Crushing the ingredients first extracts flavours that would otherwise only be released after prolonged cooking.

Method: In a large pan, combine the stock and salt, and bring to the boil. Crush the lemongrass, galangal, shallots and coriander roots. Add them to the pot. Return to the boil, then add the fish, mushrooms and kaffir lime leaves. Simmer for 8–10 minutes, or until the fish is cooked. Add the fish sauce, sugar and chillies.

Just before serving, stir in the lime juice and sprinkle with the coriander leaves. The dish should taste sour, salty and hot. Add more lime juice, fish sauce and/or chillies as needed.

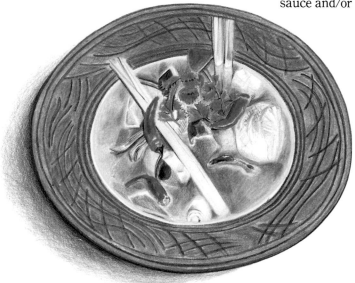

HOT AND SOUR SOUP OF GRILLED FISH

Tom Yam Pla Yang

1 banana blossom, grilled (broiled)
3 large dried chillies, deseeded and chopped
2-3 fresh small green chillies (optional)
2 cloves garlic, chopped
4 red shallots, chopped
Pinch salt
1 teaspoon kapi (shrimp paste), roasted (see glossary)
1 medium trout, salted and grilled (broiled), or 1 smoked trout
1.25 L (5 cups/2 pt) stock or water
3 stalks lemongrass, pounded
5 kaffir lime leaves, torn
30 mL (2 tablespoons) fish sauce
1 teaspoon palm sugar
15 mL (1 tablespoon) lime juice

TO MAKE THIS DISH the Thais use freshwater catfish grilled slowly over charcoal. This imparts a smoky, resinous flavour. A smoked fish could be used instead of grilling a fresh fish. A vegetarian alternative would be to substitute beancurd (tofu) for the fish and light soy sauce for the fish sauce. Mushrooms and tomatoes could also be added.

Method: Grill, broil or roast the banana blossom until the outer leaves are charred and the centre is soft when tested with a paring knife (it is similar to testing whether a potato is cooked). Cool, then peel the charred outer sheaths and quarter the white inner heart. Remove the inner core and the stamen (which are in fact the young bananas, and are very bitter) and slice the heart very finely on a bias. Wash and immerse in acidulated water.

In a mortar and pestle (or food processor), crush the dried chillies, fresh chillies (if using), garlic, shallots, salt and kapi until fine. Fillet and flake the fish very coarsely. In a large pan, bring the stock to a boil, then stir in the paste. Add the fish, lemongrass and kaffir lime leaves, then add the fish sauce, palm sugar and lime juice. Mix well and serve.

HOT AND SOUR SOUP OF PORK HOCK

Tom Yam Ka Muu

*1 pork hock (knuckle), with trotter
(foot) attached*
Water (to cover)
Salt
3 coriander (cilantro) roots
5 stalks lemongrass, pounded
*5 dried large red chillies, roasted
or grilled (broiled)*
10 kaffir lime leaves, bruised
*2 tablespoons chilli jam (see page
85)*
30 mL (2 tablespoons) fish sauce
*5-10 small fresh green chillies,
crushed*
30 mL (2 tablespoons) lime juice
*½ cup fresh coriander (cilantro)
leaves*

I LOVE THIS TYPE of soup: it is rich and complex in flavour — a combination of lemongrass and galangal, mellowed by the chilli jam and coriander, all sharpened by the addition of lime juice. This interplay, and relishing contrast of flavours, is what Thai food is all about. And to my mind it is unparalleled in other cuisines.

Method: Wash the pork hock and then grill or broil it. When charred, scrape any hair from the hock, then immerse it in water (at room temperature) for 5 minutes, allowing the skin to swell.

In a large pan bring fresh salted water to the boil (enough water to generously cover the meat), add the coriander roots and the pork hock, and simmer for about 1 hour, or until tender. Remove the pork hock and cool. Lift the meat from the bone and cut it into bite-sized pieces. Skim the fat from the stock. Return the stock to a boil, then add the lemongrass, dried chillies, kaffir lime leaves, chilli jam and pork and simmer for 2–3 minutes. Stir in the fish sauce, fresh chillies and lime juice.

Just before serving, sprinkle with the coriander leaves and check that the soup tastes hot, salty and sour. Adjust, if necessary, by adding some more fish sauce, chillies or lime juice.

SOUP OF MUSSELS AND TOMATOES

Tom Klong Hoy Malaeng Puu

*1 L (4 cups/1¾ pt) stock or salted
    water*
3 stalks lemongrass, pounded
5 slices galangal
*5 red shallots, roasted whole (see
    glossary)*
*3 cloves garlic, roasted whole (see
    glossary)*
1 kg (2 lb) mussels
2 small tomatoes, coarsely chopped
*5-10 small dried chillies, roasted
    and broken*
2-3 fresh small green chillies
15 mL (1 tablespoon) fish sauce
1 teaspoon palm sugar
*45 mL (3 tablespoons) thick
    tamarind water (see glossary)*
4 leaves pak chii farang, *shredded
    (see glossary)*

A *TOM KLONG* is a soup that is soured by fruit or vegetables, so it is important that the tomatoes used in this recipe are not too ripe. Green mango or tamarind leaves (which taste very much like sorrel) may also be used as the souring agent. Grilled or smoked fish may be substituted for the mussels.

Method: In a large pan bring the stock or salted water to the boil, then add the lemongrass (pounded first), galangal, shallots and garlic. Return to the boil, then add the mussels and tomatoes. When the mussels have opened, add the dried and fresh chillies, fish sauce, palm sugar and tamarind water.

To serve, garnish with the *pak chii farang* and check that the soup tastes sour, hot and salty. Adjust, if necessary, by adding either more tamarind water, chillies or fish sauce.

Mud Crab Soup
Tom Kha Bu Talay

250 mL (1 cup/8 fl oz) coconut
  cream
500 mL (2 cups/16 fl oz) coconut
  milk
1 stalk lemongrass, crushed
4 red shallots, bruised
10 slices young galangal
2 coriander (cilantro) roots
5 kaffir lime leaves, torn
1 teaspoon salt
1 medium mud or any soft-shelled
  crab, halved, cleaned and cut
  into serving portions
30 mL (2 tablespoons) fish sauce
30 mL (2 tablespoons) lime juice
1 tablespoon palm sugar
5–10 fresh small green chillies
¼ cup fresh coriander (cilantro)
  leaves

THIS STYLE OF SOUP is a gentler alternative to a *Tom Yam*. Its heat is mitigated by the coconut cream and it is not as sour. Westerners normally associate chicken with this soup, but as with the *Tom Yams*, it is not so limited. Any meat, poultry, seafood or vegetable may be substituted for the mud crab. Beancurd (tofu), oyster mushrooms or baby corn go particularly well if a vegetarian soup is desired.

Method: In a medium pan bring the coconut cream and milk to a boil. In a mortar and pestle or with a mallet, pound the lemongrass and shallots. Add the lemongrass, shallots, galangal, coriander roots, kaffir lime leaves, salt and crab, and simmer for about 10 minutes, or until the crab is cooked. Add the fish sauce, lime juice, palm sugar and chillies, and stir.

Just before serving, sprinkle with the coriander leaves.

TROUT WITH CARAMEL AND FISH SAUCE

Tom Kem Wan

3 cloves garlic, chopped
2 coriander (cilantro) roots
10 white peppercorns
Pinch salt
15 mL (1 tablespoon) safflower oil
3 tablespoons white (granulated)
  sugar
15 mL (1 tablespoon) water
45 mL (3 tablespoons) fish sauce
1 medium trout, cut into cutlets or
  filleted and cut into cubes
Water (to cover)
2 red shallots, sliced
2 tablespoons fresh coriander
  (cilantro) leaves

WHEN THAIS OF noble birth die, often their family publishes a memorial book recalling their life, their achievements and interests. In the case of women, this usually includes a wealth of old family recipes which were the favourite of the deceased. This recipe comes from such a book, the *Nang Seu Ngaan Sop* of Mom Ratchawong Yingdteung Sanitwongse. The original recipe calls for a *pla chorn*, a red-fleshed freshwater fish, not dissimilar to a trout.

Method: In a mortar and pestle (or in a grinder), pound the garlic, coriander roots, peppercorns and salt until fine. In a medium pan heat the oil and fry the garlic and peppercorn mixture until fragrant and beginning to colour. Add the sugar and water and stir until it caramelises. When golden, add the fish sauce and trout. Cover with water and simmer for about 5 minutes, or until cooked.

Just before serving, sprinkle with the shallots and coriander leaves.

DUCK WITH STAR ANISE AND EGGS

Bet Parlow

10 dried shiitake mushrooms
500 mL (2 cups/16 fl oz) water
30 mL (2 tablespoons) oyster sauce
1 teaspoon white (granulated)
  sugar
4 cloves garlic
3 coriander (cilantro) roots
10 white peppercorns
Pinch salt
1 tablespoon five-spice powder
3 star anise
15 mL (1 tablespoon) safflower oil
1 duck, jointed
45 mL (3 tablespoons) sweet soy sauce
3 hardboiled eggs, preferably duck,
  shelled and halved
15 mL (1 tablespoon) fish sauce
1 tablespoon palm sugar
2 tablespoons fresh coriander
  (cilantro) leaves, chopped

THIS 'STEW' IS OF Chinese origin, but has now been adapted and adopted by the Thais. Throughout all of Bangkok, which has a substantial Chinese population, there are street stalls that sell this style of soup, whether it be made with duck and mushrooms or with pork belly and beancurd (tofu), as was sold near where I lived in Bangkok. This dish is delicious when served accompanied by some steamed Chinese broccoli with oyster sauce.

Method: In a small pan soak the mushrooms in the water for 30 minutes. Add the oyster sauce and white sugar and simmer for 10–15 minutes, or until half the water has evaporated. Cool, then remove and discard the tough stems from the mushrooms, and slice caps. Reserve the mushroom stock to braise the duck.

In a mortar and pestle (or in a grinder), pound the garlic, coriander roots, peppercorns, salt, five-spice powder and star anise until fine. In a large pan heat the oil, add the pounded paste, and fry until fragrant and beginning to brown. Add the duck and soy sauce. Cook until the duck is sealed, then add the mushroom stock and enough water to cover. Add the sliced mushrooms and simmer until the duck is tender. Add the eggs, fish sauce and palm sugar, stir gently. Serve garnished with the coriander leaves.

BARRAMUNDI WITH GINGER AND TAMARIND
Tom Som Pla Grapong

½ teaspoon kapi (shrimp paste),
    roasted (see glossary) or *dried*
    prawns (shrimp)
5 red shallots
10 white peppercorns
2 coriander (cilantro) roots
2 cm (¾ in) piece ginger, chopped
Pinch salt
15 mL (1 tablespoon) safflower oil
1 clove garlic, crushed
200 g (7 oz) barramundi or *any*
    firm white-fleshed fish fillets,
    cut into 2 cm (¾ in) cubes
Water (to cover)
45 mL (3 tablespoons) thick
    tamarind water (see glossary)
1 tablespoon palm sugar
30 mL (2 tablespoons) fish sauce
2 cups (200 g/8 oz) julienned
    ginger, washed in salty water
½ bunch Chinese shallots, cut into
    2 cm (¾ in) pieces

THIS IS ANOTHER restorative, assuaging the palate after an onslaught of chillies. It is wonderful when eaten in conjunction with a very hot and pungent *Nam Prik*, such as Prawn Paste Relish (see page 109). Almost any fish or shellfish can be substituted. Beancurd (tofu) may be used instead of the fish, and light soy sauce substituted for the fish sauce.

Method: In a mortar and pestle (or food processor), crush the kapi or dried prawns, red shallots, peppercorns, coriander roots, chopped ginger and salt until fine.

In a medium pan heat the oil, add the garlic, and fry until golden. Add the paste and fry until fragrant. Add the fish and continue to fry for about 5 minutes, or until it is sealed. When the fish is almost cooked, add water to cover. Add the tamarind water, palm sugar, fish sauce and julienned ginger, and simmer for 2–3 minutes, or until the fish is cooked and flavours are combined.

Just before serving add the Chinese shallots. The soup should taste sour, salty and sweet, and fragrant from the ginger. Add more tamarind water, fish sauce and/or palm sugar as needed.

OMELETTE SOUP

Gaeng Jeut Kai Jiaw

30 mL (2 tablespoons) safflower oil
2 cloves garlic, minced
2 eggs
Pinch salt
2 pickling onions, finely sliced
500 mL (2 cups/16 fl oz) chicken
  stock
30 mL (2 tablespoons) oyster sauce
1 teaspoon palm sugar
100 g (4 oz) bean sprouts
2 tablespoons fresh coriander
  (cilantro) leaves
½ teaspoon white peppercorns,
  ground

ONLY THE THAIS would come up with a fried-egg soup! Often pork balls, made from minced pork and seasoned with salt and white pepper, are added to this soup.

Method: Heat the oil in a wok, add the garlic and fry until light golden in colour; drain and retain the oil.

Break the eggs into a bowl and beat them together with the salt. Just before cooking, add the onion. Reheat the oil in the wok over a high heat and add the egg mixture. Cook the omelette until the edges have set and then turn it and drain. Allow it to cool and then cut it into bite-sized pieces.

In a medium pan bring the stock to the boil, add the oyster sauce, palm sugar, omelette pieces and bean sprouts. Serve immediately, sprinkled with the garlic, coriander and white peppercorns.

CHICKEN AND SIAMESE WATERCRESS SOUP

Gaeng Jeut Gai Sy Pak Bung

3 red shallots
Pinch salt
1 coriander (cilantro) root
5 white peppercorns
500 mL (2 cups/16 fl oz) chicken
*   or pork stock*
30 mL (2 tablespoons) Thai yellow
*   bean sauce*
1 teaspoon oyster sauce
1 teaspoon palm sugar
100 g (4 oz) chicken thigh fillets,
*   thinly sliced*
1 bunch Siamese watercress, cut
*   into 5 cm (2 in) lengths*

THIS IS A LOVELY, gentle soup that can be used to counterbalance the heat from a green curry. If Siamese watercress is unavailable, then spinach or watercress could be substituted.

Method: In a mortar and pestle (or food processor), crush the shallots with the salt, coriander root and peppercorns.

In a medium pan bring the stock to a boil and add the paste, bean sauce, oyster sauce and palm sugar. Add the chicken and simmer for about 3 minutes, or until the chicken is just cooked. Add the Siamese watercress and simmer until it wilts. Serve immediately.

PORK RIBS AND BAMBOO SOUP

Gaeng Jeut Graduk Muu Nor Mai

1 medium (about 300 g/10 oz)
    bamboo stalk
500 mL (2 cups/16 fl oz) chicken
    stock
200 g (7 oz) pork ribs
    (tips and cartilage) cut into
    3 cm (1½ in) pieces
1 bunch Asian celery
100 g (4 oz) oyster mushrooms
30 mL (2 tablespoons) oyster sauce
1 teaspoon white peppercorns,
    ground
2 tablespoons fresh coriander
    (cilantro) leaves

THE SUCCESS OF this soup lies in the somewhat bitter flavour of the bamboo. This is very much a peasant soup, where a minimum of technique is required, but the flavour combination is anything but coarse. This soup with some Prawn Paste Relish (see page 109) and a thick red curry make a wonderful combination.

Method: Peel and finely slice the bamboo stalk; wash it and then blanch it in boiling salted water; drain and refresh. Bring some fresh salted water to the boil, then add the blanched bamboo and simmer it for about 10 minutes, or until tender and not too bitter.

In a medium pan bring the stock to a boil. Add the pork ribs and simmer for about 20 minutes, or until tender, skimming regularly to remove fat. Add the bamboo, celery, mushrooms and oyster sauce and simmer for 3 minutes.

To serve, sprinkle with the peppercorns and coriander.

CHINESE BITTER MELON STUFFED WITH PORK SOUP

Gaeng Jeut Mara Sort Sy

*2 Chinese bitter melons, cut into
   2 cm (¾ in) rounds and
   deseeded*
2 tablespoons salt
2 cloves garlic, chopped
5 white peppercorns
1 coriander (cilantro) root
Pinch salt
150 g (5 oz) pork, minced (ground)
*1 teaspoon white (granulated)
   sugar*
500 mL (2 cups/16 fl oz) stock
1 teaspoon palm sugar
*4 Chinese shallots, cut into 2 cm
   (¾ in) lengths*
*2 cloves garlic, minced and deep-
   fried*
15 mL (1 tablespoon) fish sauce
15 mL (1 tablespoon) oyster sauce
*1 teaspoon white peppercorns,
   ground*
*1 tablespoon coriander (cilantro)
   leaves*

THIS SOUP IS of Chinese origin, bitterness not being a taste characteristic of Thai food. Prawns may be added to this soup to sweeten the flavour. If you find Chinese melon is too bitter, then you can substitute cucumbers. In this case there is no need to salt or pre-blanch the vegetable.

Method: Cover the rounds of melon with 2 tablespoons of salt and set aside for 2 hours. Rinse off the salt and blanch the melon once or twice depending on taste and the bitterness of the melon.

In a mortar and pestle (or food processor), pound the chopped garlic, whole peppercorns, coriander root and salt until fine. Combine with the pork and white sugar. Stuff the melon with the pork mixture.

In a medium pan bring the stock to a boil and simmer for about 10 minutes, or until the pork stuffing is cooked. Stir in the palm sugar, shallots, garlic, fish sauce and oyster sauce.

Serve sprinkled with the ground white peppercorns and coriander.

PUMPKIN IN COCONUT MILK WITH DRIED PRAWNS

Tom Gati Fak Thong

*100 g (½ cup/4 oz) dried prawns
  (shrimp) or 100 g (½ cup/4 oz)
  small green prawns (raw
  shrimp), peeled and deveined*
Pinch salt
*½ teaspoon kapi (shrimp paste),
  roasted (see glossary, optional)*
*1 tablespoon dried prawns
  (shrimp), extra*
3 red shallots, chopped
10 white peppercorns
*500 mL (2 cups/16 fl oz) coconut
  cream mixed with coconut milk*
*200 g (7 oz) pumpkin (squash),
  cleaned and cut into 2 cm
  (¾ in) thick slices*
Pinch palm sugar
15 mL (1 tablespoon) fish sauce

THIS SOUP PERFECTLY counterbalances the richness of a stir fry with chilli paste or a pungent *Nam Prik*.

Method: Soak the ½ cup of dried prawns in water for 20 minutes; drain.

In a mortar and pestle (or food processor), crush the salt, kapi (if using), the extra tablespoon of dried prawns, shallots and white peppercorns until fine.

In a medium pan bring the coconut cream and milk to the boil, add the paste and stir to dissolve. Add the pumpkin and the rehydrated prawns and simmer 10–15 minutes, or until the pumpkin is tender. Add the palm sugar and fish sauce. If using fresh prawns, add them to the soup when the pumpkin is tender. Simmer until the prawns are cooked, about 2 minutes. It may be necessary to moisten the soup with some water or extra coconut milk, if too much of the liquid has evaporated. Reheat and serve.

STEAMED CHICKEN SOUP

Tum Gai

500 mL (2 cups/16 fl oz) chicken
    stock
1 teaspoon salt
1 tablespoon palm sugar
45 mL (3 tablespoons) oyster sauce
2 teaspoons Chinese rice wine
2 star anise
3 slices ginger, 2.5 cm (1 in)
    in size
2 cloves garlic, unpeeled
2 coriander (cilantro) roots
50 g (2 oz) pork trotter (pigs' feet)
    or *pork skin, blanched*
    (optional)
3 chicken thighs, trimmed, washed
    and cut into thirds
1 bottle gourd or *any gourd or*
    cucumber, peeled, deseeded, and
    cut into 2 cm (¾ in) cubes
½ teaspoon white peppercorns,
    ground
2 tablespoons coriander (cilantro)
    leaves

THERE IS AN old Chinese restaurant just near Lumpini Park in Bangkok that specialises in this style of soup. Huge steamers line the entrance, where the customer can choose what they would like to eat. Pork with pickled greens, tripe with Chinese spices, or chicken with Chinese mushrooms are among the selection. Gentle and soothing, this soup would be delicious with the *Lon Kapi* (Kapi Paste Simmered in Coconut Cream, see page 115). Whatever meat you choose to use, ensure that it can sustain prolonged cooking.

Method: In a medium pan bring the stock to the boil, add the salt, palm sugar, oyster sauce, wine, star anise, ginger, garlic, coriander roots and pork trotter, and simmer for about 10 minutes, skimming the stock scrupulously. Place the chicken and the gourd in a large heatproof bowl and strain the stock over it. Cover with foil, place the bowl in a steamer and steam for about 1 hour or until the chicken is cooked. Serve in the bowl, sprinkled with the pepper and coriander leaves.

STEAMED DISHES

STEAMED EGGS

Kai Tum

1 clove garlic
2 coriander (cilantro) roots
5 white peppercorns
Pinch salt
100 g (4 oz) pork, minced (ground)
3 eggs
30 mL (2 tablespoons) water
2 Chinese shallots, peeled and
   chopped
3 stalks Asian celery, chopped
1 tablespoon fresh coriander
   (cilantro) leaves

THIS IS A very gentle dish and makes an ideal accompaniment to very hot curries, such as *Gaeng Som Pla Tua Fak Yaew* (Sour Orange Curry with Snake Beans, see page 58), *Gaeng Gwiow Wan* (Green Curry of Pork, see page 50) or *Gaeng Leuang* (Yellow Curry, see page 59).

Method: In a mortar and pestle (or food processor), crush the garlic, coriander roots, white peppercorns and salt until fine. Mix this paste with the pork, then combine with the eggs, water, shallots and celery. Pour this mixture into a large heatproof soup bowl, place the bowl in a steamer and steam on a gentle heat for about 20 minutes or until the custard has set. Serve the custard in its mould, sprinkled with the coriander leaves.

SNAPPER WITH GINGER

Pla Bae Sae

1 savoy cabbage leaf
200 g (7 oz) snapper (sea bass)
*   fillets, cubed*
4 cloud's ear mushrooms (if dried,
*   rehydrate in warm water for*
*   20 minutes), sliced*
2 tablespoons julienned ginger
2 pickling onions, finely sliced
200 mL (1 scant cup/7 fl oz)
*   chicken stock*
15 mL (1 tablespoon) fish sauce
15 mL (1 tablespoon) oyster sauce
1 teaspoon palm sugar
1 teaspoon white peppercorns,
*   ground*
2 tablespoons coriander (cilantro)
*   leaves*

COOKED IN THIS MANNER, any delicate fish remains moist, tender and succulent. It is a perfect foil for a searingly hot curry, such as a green curry (see page 50), or a *Nam Prik* (Prawn Paste Relish, see page 109).

Method: Line a medium heatproof bowl with the cabbage leaf, then add the fish, mushrooms, ginger and onions. Bring the stock to the boil, then add the fish sauce, oyster sauce and palm sugar. Pour the stock over the fish, place the bowl in a steamer, and steam for about 10 minutes or until the fish is cooked. Serve sprinkled with pepper and coriander.

WRASSE WITH CHILLIES AND LIME JUICE
Pla Neung

1 coriander (cilantro) root

1 teaspoon salt

4 cloves garlic

4–10 fresh small green chillies

45 mL (3 tablespoons) lime juice

1 tablespoon castor (superfine)
*   sugar*

30 mL (2 tablespoons) fish sauce

1 medium wrasse or *any firm,*
*   white sea fish*

THE WRASSE IS one of the most popular saltwater fish in Asia, appreciated for its soft and yielding texture. The way that the Thais would treat such a delicate fish is to steam it, dressing it with this not-so-delicate sauce. Parrot fish, red snapper or any white-fleshed fish could be used successfully. Scoring the fish enables faster and more even cooking.

Method: In a mortar and pestle (or food processor), crush the coriander root, salt and garlic until fine, then add the chillies, lime juice, sugar and fish sauce. Stir or blend until the sugar dissolves.

Wash and score the fish, place on a heatproof plate small enough to fit into the steamer and cover with the sauce. Steam the fish for about 10–15 minutes or until it is cooked. Serve immediately.

BLACK BREAM WITH GINGER AND CHINESE SHALLOTS

Pla Neung King Ton Horm

1 medium black bream or *use sea bream, sole, snapper, sea bass or sea perch*

15 mL (1 tablespoon) oyster sauce

100 g (4 oz) ginger, julienned

4 Chinese shallots, finely sliced

15 mL (1 tablespoon) Chinese rice wine

15 mL (1 tablespoon) soy sauce

2 fresh long green chillies, deseeded and julienned

2 tablespoons coriander (cilantro) sprigs

5 white peppercorns, ground

45 mL (3 tablespoons) safflower oil (include a little sesame oil and, if possible, some oil that has previously been used for deep-frying either shallots or garlic)

THIS RECIPE ADMITTEDLY would not be out of place in a Chinese cookbook, although that certainly doesn't stop the adaptable Thais from calling this version their own. The technique of pouring hot oil over the cooked fish and the raw julienne serves to cook the garnish and anoint the fish with the now-flavoured oil. Any white-fleshed fish can be used.

Method: Wash the fish, then smear it with oyster sauce. Steam the fish for about 10 minutes or until cooked, then transfer it to a serving plate. Cover the fish with the ginger, shallots, wine, soy sauce, chillies, coriander and white pepper. In a small saucepan heat the oil until it is almost smoking, pour it over the fish and serve.

FRESHWATER PERCH WITH PICKLED PLUMS

Pla Neung Buai

5 dried shiitake mushrooms
250 mL (1 cup/8 fl oz) water
15 mL (1 tablespoon) oyster sauce
1 teaspoon palm sugar
1 freshwater perch or redfin, about
    250 g (8 oz)
1 teaspoon salt
100 g (4 oz) ginger, julienned
50 g (2 oz) Asian celery, cut into
    2 cm (¾ in) lengths
2 cloves garlic, finely sliced
    lengthways
4 pickled plums, pitted and sliced
30 mL (2 tablespoons) brine from
    pickled plums
30 mL (2 tablespoons) chicken
    stock
15 mL (1 tablespoon) fish sauce
1 tablespoon coriander (cilantro)
    leaves
10 white peppercorns, ground

AROUND CHIANG MAI where I first had this dish, there are many *Baan Suan* — restaurants set in gardens. They are well regarded by the Thais, who often consider a restaurant's atmosphere is just as important as its food. Up country, atmosphere means live entertainment and live entertainment means a motley collection of hacks accompanying a rambunctiously second-rate chanteuse. I loved it, and the food was just as good as its atmosphere.

Method: Rehydrate the mushrooms for 20 minutes in the water. Bring to the boil, add the oyster sauce and palm sugar, then simmer for 5 minutes. Cool, destem and finely slice the mushrooms.

Wash and score the fish, rub with the salt, then place in a deep-sided steaming plate. Cover with the ginger, celery, garlic, pickled plums, their brine, the mushrooms and their stock, the chicken stock and fish sauce. Steam for about 15–20 minutes or until the fish is cooked. The broth will taste salty and sour, and be fragrant from the ginger and mushrooms. Garnish with the coriander leaves and pepper, and serve.

STUFFED SQUID

Pla Meuk Yort Sy Neung

15 medium squid
2 cloves garlic
2 coriander (cilantro) roots
10 white peppercorns
1 teaspoon salt
100 g (4 oz) pork, minced (ground)
100 g (4 oz) prawns (shrimp),
*   minced (ground)*
1 teaspoon white (granulated)
*   sugar*
1 teaspoon fish sauce
1 egg
2 tablespoons coriander (cilantro)
*   leaves, chopped*

BE CAREFUL WHEN filling the squid as it could explode if it is overfilled or steamed over too high a heat. As an interesting variation, the squid could be grilled, broiled or substituted for the fish in Trout with Caramel and Fish Sauce (see page 67). Serve with a bowl of fish sauce mixed with chopped chillies, sliced red shallots and sliced lime.

Method: Skin and clean the squid, keeping the body whole and retaining the legs.

In a mortar and pestle (or a food processor), pound the garlic, coriander roots, peppercorns and salt until fine. In a bowl combine the pork and prawn mince and incorporate the paste, sugar, fish sauce and egg. Stuff the squid with this mixture and steam over a low heat for about 10–15 minutes or until cooked. Sprinkle with the coriander and serve.

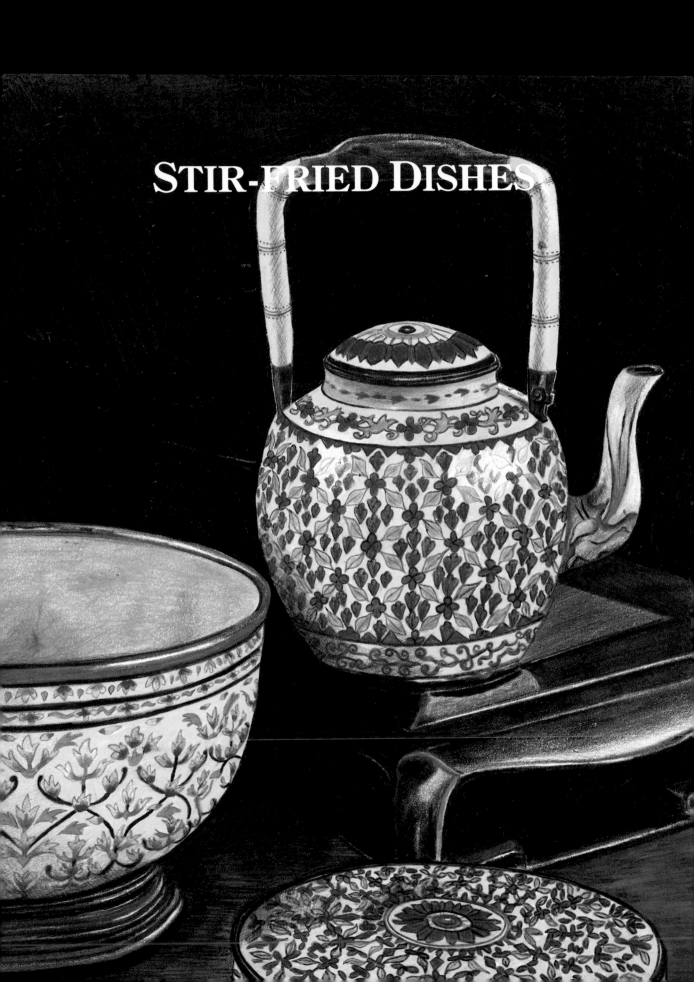

STIR-FRIED DISHES

CRAB WITH CURRY POWDER

Bpu Ma Pat Pong Garee

30 mL (2 tablespoons) safflower oil
2 cloves garlic, chopped
1½ tablespoons curry powder (see
　glossary)
250 mL (1 cup/8 fl oz) coconut
　cream
1 crab weighing 300 g (10 oz),
　halved, cleaned and cut into
　6 pieces
2 pickling onions, cut in half, then
　finely sliced lengthways
30 mL (2 tablespoons) fish sauce
1 teaspoon palm sugar
100 g (4 oz) Chinese shallots,
　peeled and cut into 3 cm (1 in)
　lengths, or 1 bunch Asian
　celery, cut into 3 cm (1 in)
　lengths
2 tablespoons fresh coriander
　(cilantro) leaves
1 teaspoon white peppercorns,
　ground
5 red shallots, sliced lengthways
　and deep-fried (see glossary,
　optional)

THE SUCCESS OF this dish relies on the freshness of the curry powder — ensure that a good quality one is used or, even better, make your own. Any small crab, such as a soft-shelled crab, blue crab, spider crab or blue swimmer crab may be used.

Method: Heat the oil in a wok, add the garlic and fry until golden. Add the curry powder and, stirring regularly, cook the curry for about 2 minutes, or until fragrant. Do not allow it to scorch. Add the coconut cream, crab, onions, fish sauce and sugar, cover with a lid and simmer for about 7–10 minutes, or until the crab is cooked. Mix in the shallots or celery. Serve sprinkled with the coriander, white pepper and shallots, if using.

CLAMS WITH CHILLI JAM

Hoi Lay Pat Nam Prik Pao

250 mL (1 cup/8 fl oz) coconut
   cream
4 tablespoons of the chilli jam
500 g (1 lb) clams or any mollusc
15 mL (1 tablespoon) fish sauce
1 tablespoon palm sugar
5 kaffir lime leaves, torn
3 fresh long red or green chillies,
   cut in half and deseeded
20–25 fresh Thai basil leaves

CHILLI JAM
1 L (4 cups/1¾ pt) safflower oil
500 g (4 cups/1 lb) red shallots,
   sliced lengthways
250 g (2 cups/8 oz) garlic, sliced
   lengthways
1 cup dried prawns (shrimp),
   rinsed and dried
10 dried long red chillies, deseeded
   and chopped
250 g (1 cup/8 oz) palm sugar
125 mL (½ cup/4 fl oz) thick
   tamarind water (see glossary)
1 tablespoon salt
45 mL (3 tablespoons) fish sauce

CHILLI JAM IS a versatile paste that is constantly called for in cooking Thai soups, salads or stir-fries. Although the quantities given here may seem excessive, it is in fact easier to make the jam in these large amounts. Chilli jam keeps indefinitely and it really is convenient to have a supply in the refrigerator ready for use. Any fish, meat or vegetable may be used instead of clams.

Method: In a medium pan, boil the coconut cream 3–5 minutes until it separates. Add the chilli jam and cook for 2–3 minutes or until fragrant. Add the clams and continue cooking for 3–5 minutes, or until the clams begin to open. Mix in the remaining ingredients and remove from the heat. Serve with the chilli jam.

To make the chilli jam, in a wok heat the oil and separately deep-fry the shallots and garlic until golden. Add the prawns and chillies and deep-fry for 30 seconds or until fragrant; drain. Purée the deep-fried ingredients together in a food processor, moistening with 250 mL (1 cup/8 fl oz) oil from the deep-frying to facilitate the blending. Transfer the purée to a medium pot, bring to the boil, then add the palm sugar, tamarind water, salt and fish sauce. Simmer, stirring regularly, for about 5 minutes, or until quite thick and tasting sweet, sour and salty. Store in an airtight container.

SQUID WITH CHILLIES AND BASIL

Pla Meuk Pat Prik

3-10 small green chillies
2 fresh long red chillies, deseeded
4 cloves garlic
2 coriander (cilantro) roots
Pinch salt
30 mL (2 tablespoons) safflower oil
6 squid, cleaned and skinned
3 banana chillies, cut in half and
    deseeded
35 mL (2 tablespoons) fish sauce
1 tablespoon palm sugar
3 kaffir lime leaves, torn
20-25 fresh Thai basil leaves

IF MORE HEAT is desired do not scrape out the chilli seeds. Chicken or pork ribs could be substituted for the squid.

Method: In a mortar and pestle (or a food processor), coarsely crush together the chillies, garlic, coriander roots and salt. Heat the oil in a wok, add the paste and fry over a high heat for 2–3 minutes, or until fragrant. Add the squid and chillies and stir-fry for about 3 minutes or until cooked. Add the fish sauce, palm sugar, kaffir lime leaves and basil.

Just before serving, check that it tastes hot, salty and sweet. Add more chillies, fish sauce and/or palm sugar if necessary.

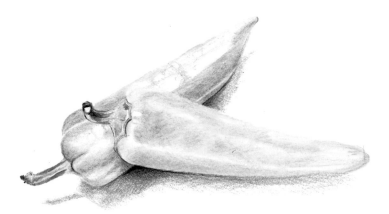

PORK WITH SNAKE BEANS AND CHILLI PASTE

Pat Prik King Tua Fak Yaew

*30 mL (2 tablespoons) safflower oil
or 60 mL (4 tablespoons) if
using pork ribs or leg*

2 cloves garlic, crushed

*200 g (7 oz) pork belly, fresh bacon
or pork ribs or leg, steamed and
sliced into small strips*

3 tablespoons of the chilli paste

30 mL (2 tablespoons) fish sauce

*1 tablespoon white (granulated)
sugar*

*50 g (2 oz) snake (long green)
beans, cut into 3 cm (1¼ in)
lengths*

6 kaffir lime leaves, shredded

*3 fresh large red chillies, halved
and deseeded*

CHILLI PASTE

*5-10 dried red long chillies,
deseeded and chopped*

3 red shallots, chopped

2 cloves garlic

½ stalk lemongrass, sliced

*1 teaspoon galangal, peeled and
chopped*

3 coriander (cilantro) roots

*1 tablespoon dried prawns
(shrimp), rinsed*

1 teaspoon salt

THIS IS A pungent dish. One very old recipe calls for the use of *Kai Kem* (Salty Eggs, see page 116) instead of pork.

Method: In a medium pan, heat the oil, add the garlic and fry until golden. Add the pork and fry until it begins to colour. Add the chilli paste and fry for about 5-8 minutes or until fragrant; if necessary, moisten with a little water to prevent the paste from catching. Add the fish sauce and sugar. Mix in the beans, kaffir lime leaves and chillies, fry for a further 2-3 minutes, or until the beans are cooked. It will taste quite rich and salty. Serve immediately.

To make the chilli paste, purée all of the ingredients in a food processor, using as little water as possible, until fine.

CUCUMBER AND PORK WITH EGG

Taeng Gwaa Pat Muu Sy Kai

15 mL (1 tablespoon) safflower oil
2 cloves garlic, crushed with a
*   pinch of salt*
100 g (4 oz) pork belly or fresh
*   bacon, steamed and cut into*
*   2 cm (¾ in) cubes*
1 small cucumber, roll cut (see
*   glossary)*
2 eggs, beaten
15 mL (1 tablespoon) fish sauce
1 teaspoon white (granulated)
*   sugar*
2 tablespoons fresh coriander
*   (cilantro) leaves*
1 teaspoon white peppercorns,
*   ground*

THIS IS QUITE delicious when eaten with *Nam Prik Kapi* (Prawn Paste Relish, see page 109). As an alternative, substitute pumpkin and prawns for the cucumber and pork.

Method: In a wok heat the oil over a high heat, add the salted garlic and fry until it begins to colour. Add the pork and fry for 4 minutes over a high heat. Add the cucumber and fry for about 3 minutes, or until the cucumber begins to turn translucent. Add the eggs and cook for a further 3 minutes, then add the fish sauce and sugar, stir for a few moments until dissolved. Serve sprinkled with the coriander and ground white peppercorns.

CRAB WITH BEAN SPROUTS AND EGG

Bpu Pat Kai Sy Tua Nork

2 cloves garlic
Pinch salt
30 mL (2 tablespoons) safflower oil
2 eggs, chicken or duck, lightly
   beaten
100 g (4 oz) crab meat
15 mL (1 tablespoon) oyster sauce
1 teaspoon castor (superfine) sugar
30 mL (2 tablespoons) stock
50 g (2 oz) bean sprouts
¼ teaspoon white peppercorns,
   ground
1 tablespoon fresh coriander
   (cilantro) leaves

THIS IS A delightful lunchtime dish, usually eaten with a bowl of rice and bamboo and pork soup.

Method: Crush the garlic and salt together. Heat the oil in a pan and brown the salted garlic. When golden, add the eggs and fry until partially cooked. Add the crab, oyster sauce, sugar and stock. When the liquid has come to the boil, add the bean sprouts and fold the egg mixture over them. Serve sprinkled with the white pepper and coriander leaves.

CLOUD'S EAR MUSHROOMS WITH YOUNG GINGER

Pat King Het Huu Nuu

30 mL (2 tablespoons) safflower oil
2 cloves garlic, crushed with a
    pinch of salt
20 cloud's ear mushrooms
100 g (4 oz) young ginger,
    julienned (if only mature ginger
    is available, then rinse in salted
    water to reduce its pungency)
4 Chinese shallots, peeled and cut
    into 3 cm (1¼ in) lengths
100 g (4 oz) small prawns
    (shrimp), cleaned
15 mL (1 tablespoon) fish sauce
Pinch white (granulated) sugar

IF FRESH CLOUD'S ear mushrooms are unobtainable, then buy the dehydrated ones from a Chinese food store, rinse them in water and then soak in fresh water for 20 minutes. Rinse once more before using. Any mushrooms would make a satisfactory alternative to cloud's ears.

Method: In a wok, heat the oil over a high heat, add the salted garlic and fry until golden. Add the mushrooms, ginger, shallots and prawns, and fry for about 3 minutes, or until the prawns are cooked. Add the fish sauce and sugar. Remove from the heat and serve.

STIR-FRIED BEAN SPROUTS

Pat Tua Nork Sawai

30 mL (2 tablespoons) safflower oil

*2 cloves garlic, crushed with a
   pinch of salt*

*50 g (2 oz) pork fillet or tenderloin,
   finely sliced*

*50 g (2 oz) small prawns (shrimp),
   shelled and deveined*

*100 g (4 oz) bean sprouts, topped
   and tailed*

*100 g (4 oz) Chinese (garlic) chives,
   cut into 3 cm (1¼ in) lengths*

15 mL (1 tablespoon) fish sauce

*1 teaspoon white (granulated)
   sugar*

*1 teaspoon white peppercorns,
   ground*

*2 tablespoons fresh coriander
   (cilantro) leaves*

IT IS IMPORTANT to add the bean sprouts at the last moment to ensure that they are still crisp. If a vegetarian dish is desired, the pork fillet and prawns may be omitted.

Method: In a wok, heat the oil over a high heat, add the salted garlic and fry until golden. Add the pork and prawns and fry over a high heat for about 3 minutes, or until the prawns are cooked. Add the bean sprouts, chives, fish sauce and sugar. Serve sprinkled with the white peppercorns and coriander.

BEANCURD WITH ASIAN CELERY

Tor Huu Pat Keun Chai

30 mL (2 tablespoons) safflower oil

*2 cloves garlic, crushed with a
    pinch of salt*

*1 bunch (about 100 g/4 oz) Asian
    celery (discard any yellowing
    leaves and keep the roots for
    making stock)*

*100 g (4 oz) soft beancurd (tofu),
    rinsed in water*

30 mL (2 tablespoons) oyster sauce

30 mL (2 tablespoons) stock or
    water

*1 teaspoon white (granulated)
    sugar*

ALWAYS USE THE soft-textured variety of beancurd — its silken texture contrasts with the crispness of the celery. There is no need to chop the beancurd in this recipe as the action of stir-frying will break it up.

Method: In a wok heat the oil over a high heat, add the salted garlic and fry until golden. Add the celery and fry until it wilts, then add the beancurd and oyster sauce. Add the stock or water, and the sugar, and stir. Remove from the heat and serve.

SIAMESE WATERCRESS WITH YELLOW BEANS AND GARLIC
Pat Pak Bung Fy Daeng

2 cloves garlic, crushed

2-5 fresh small red chillies

1 bunch Siamese watercress, cut into 3 cm (1¼ in) lengths (discard the hard stalks at the end of the bunch and any yellowing leaves)

15 mL (1 tablespoon) Thai yellow bean sauce

15 mL (1 tablespoon) oyster sauce

1 teaspoon white (granulated) sugar

10-12 fresh Thai basil leaves

30 mL (2 tablespoons) safflower oil

THIS STIR-FRY IS a favourite of the Thais. Often they crumble a little roasted kapi (shrimp paste) and a few dried prawns (shrimp) into this dish. In the provincial capital of Phitsanulok, there are several riverside food stalls, one of which has become famous for the manner in which it serves its watercress. After cooking the watercress in a wok, the cook runs across the road and flings the vegetable at the hapless customer, who attempts to catch it on his or her plate — sometimes not so successfully. Any green vegetable can be used — spinach or asparagus is especially delicious. Siamese watercress is often called *ong choy* or *kang kong* or water spinach. Ordinary spinach makes a happy substitute.

Method: Crush the garlic and chillies and transfer to a bowl. Stir in the watercress, yellow bean sauce, oyster sauce, sugar and basil. In a wok heat the oil until smoking, then add the watercress mixture and stir-fry for about 1–2 minutes, or until the watercress has wilted. Serve immediately.

OCEAN PERCH WITH THREE-FLAVOURED SAUCE

Pla Tort Sahm Rot

4 cloves garlic

*4 long fresh red or green chillies,
    cut in half and deseeded*

2 coriander (cilantro) roots

1 teaspoon salt

30 mL (2 tablespoons) safflower oil

*3 tablespoons white (granulated)
    sugar*

*30 mL (2 tablespoons) tamarind
    water (see glossary)*

30 mL (2 tablespoons) fish sauce

125 mL (½ cup/4 fl oz) water

*1.5 L (6 cups/2½ pt) safflower oil
    for deep-frying*

*1 large ocean perch, redfish or rock
    fish or any firm white-fleshed
    fish, scored and rubbed with salt*

*2 tablespoons fresh coriander
    (cilantro) leaves*

I FIRST HAD this dish at Hua Hin, a resort town three hours south of Bangkok. Here, on the pier, is one of the best seafood restaurants in Thailand. It is highly regarded not so much for the standard of the cooking — as everything is dealt with simply — but for the extraordinary freshness of the ingredients, which come to shore within sight of the restaurant.

Method: In a mortar and pestle (or a food processor), crush together the garlic, chillies, coriander roots and salt. Heat the oil in a small pan and fry the paste for 2–3 minutes or until fragrant. Add the sugar, tamarind water, fish sauce and water, and simmer for 5 minutes.

Heat the deep-frying oil in a wok or, even better, a deep-frier, add the fish and fry over a high heat for about 10 minutes, or until cooked.

To serve, place the fish on a plate, pour over the sauce and sprinkle with coriander leaves.

MACKEREL WITH CHILLI SAUCE

Pla Tuu Chut Blaeng Tort

1 L (4 cups/1¾ pt) safflower oil
200 g (7 oz) mackerel fillets

BATTER
50 g (½ cup/2 oz) rice flour
2 tablespoons arrowroot flour
1 teaspoon salt
125 mL (½ cup/4 fl oz) water
30 mL (2 tablespoons) coconut
    cream

CHILLI SAUCE
2 large fresh red chillies, deseeded
    and chopped
4 cloves garlic
3 coriander (cilantro) roots
2 teaspoons salt
250 g (1 cup/8 oz) white
    (granulated) sugar
125 mL (½ cup/4 fl oz) Thai
    coconut vinegar
125 mL (½ cup/4 fl oz) water
15 mL (1 tablespoon) fish sauce
2 tablespoons fresh coriander
    (cilantro) leaves

TRADITIONALLY THE THAIS would use a small fish they call *pla tuu*, a little mackerel that is their favourite fish. In all the markets throughout Thailand one can see small bamboo steamers filled with this fish. It is eaten with *Nam Prik*, in *Miangs* and in salads. It has a very oily and pronounced taste. Western mackerel, of course, can be substituted for *pla tuu*.

Method: Heat the oil in a wok, then dip the fish into the batter and deep-fry over a medium heat for about 5 minutes or until golden.

To make the batter, sift both the flours and salt into a bowl. Whisk in the water and coconut cream. Allow to rest for 30 minutes, and if it is too thick moisten it with an extra 15–30 mL (1–2 tablespoons) of water.

To make the chilli sauce, in a mortar and pestle (or a food processor), crush together the chillies, garlic, coriander roots and salt. Transfer the paste to a small pan and stir in the sugar, vinegar and water. Simmer for 5 minutes, then add the fish sauce. Serve sprinkled with the coriander leaves in a small bowl.

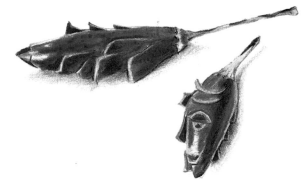

CRISPY FRIED PORK

Muu Grop

4 cloves garlic
1 tablespoon salt
15 white peppercorns
2 coriander (cilantro) roots
1 kg (2 lb) pork belly (fresh bacon)
125 mL (½ cup/4 fl oz) Thai
   coconut vinegar
4 tablespoons salt
1 L (4 cups/1¾ pt) safflower oil for
   deep-frying
4 tablespoons chilli jam (see page
   85)
½ cup fresh coriander (cilantro)
   leaves
½ small cucumber, halved
   lengthways and finely sliced

THIS SHOULD REALLY only be made by those who have great self-discipline. To those who have any weakness for pork or for deep-fried foods, let me issue this caveat: double the quantities!

Method: In a mortar and pestle (or a food processor), crush together the garlic, salt, peppercorns and coriander roots until fine. Marinate the pork in this mixture for at least 2 hours, then steam for 30 minutes or until the pork is tender. Cool and cut into 3 cm (1¼ in) wide lengths. Score the pork skin with a sharp knife across the length of the strips. Brush the skin with the vinegar and allow to dry. Repeat this process three more times, and then rub with the salt. Allow to dry out completely in a low oven for 3 hours.

Heat the oil in a wok or deep-frier until hot but not smoking, add the pork strips and deep-fry for about 5 minutes, or until the skin has crackled and is golden. Slice the strips crossways and serve with the chilli jam, coriander leaves and cucumber.

QUAIL WITH GARLIC AND PEPPERCORNS
Nok Grata Tort Gratiam Prik Thai

1.5 L (6 cups/2½ pt) safflower oil
  for deep-frying
2 large quail, cleaned, quartered
  and marinated in 30 mL
  (2 tablespoons) sweet soy sauce
  overnight
2 tablespoons coriander (cilantro)
  leaves

GARLIC MIX
3 coriander (cilantro) roots
Pinch salt
20 white peppercorns
½ slice ginger
2 heads of garlic, unpeeled

CHILLI AND VINEGAR SAUCE
3 large fresh red chillies, deseeded
  and chopped
1 coriander (cilantro) root
4 cloves garlic
2 teaspoons salt
30 mL (2 tablespoons) Thai
  coconut vinegar
1 tablespoon castor (superfine)
  sugar

ON EVERY THAI menu there is at least one item that is deep-fried with garlic and peppercorns. It is a delicious way of dressing food. Any meat, fish or vegetable that can sustain deep-frying can be treated this way. The garlic, coriander root and white peppercorn mixture is one of the most ancient spice combinations in Thai food, and it is found in marinades, in curry pastes, in stir-fries and soups. This taste, along with chillies, lime juice, fish sauce, sugar and kapi (shrimp paste), is the fundamental seasoning basis of Thai dishes.

To make this a vegetarian dish, four long green eggplants (aubergines), available from South-east Asian food stores, may be substituted for the quail.

Method: Heat the oil in a wok until almost smoking, then carefully add the quail and the garlic mix. Fry for about 5 minutes, or until golden. Strain the birds and rest them for 2–3 minutes before serving. Serve with the chilli and vinegar sauce and coriander leaves.

To make the garlic mix, in a mortar and pestle (or a food processor), crush the coriander roots with the salt and peppercorns. When well pounded, add the ginger and garlic. Continue to pound until well mixed.

To make the chilli and vinegar sauce, in a mortar and pestle (or a food processor), crush together the chillies, coriander root, garlic and salt until fine. Add the coconut vinegar and sugar. The flavour will be quite pronounced — sour, salty and sweet, all at once.

EGGS WITH SWEET FISH SAUCE

Kai Luuk Koey

250 g (1 cup/8 oz) palm sugar

75 mL (5 tablespoons) fish sauce

30 mL (2 tablespoons) tamarind water (see glossary)

1 L (4 cups/1¾ pt) safflower oil for deep-frying

6 eggs, hardboiled and shelled

5 red shallots, finely sliced lengthways and deep-fried (see glossary)

3 cloves garlic, finely sliced lengthways and deep-fried (see glossary)

6 small dried red chillies, roasted or deep-fried

4 tablespoons fresh coriander (cilantro) leaves, chopped

THESE ARE PEJORATIVELY called son-in-law eggs in Thai.

Method: In a small pan, combine the palm sugar, fish sauce and tamarind water, and simmer until the sugar has dissolved. Skim if necessary. Check that it tastes sweet, salty and slightly sour. Adjust by adding more palm sugar, fish sauce and/or tamarind water if necessary. Heat the oil in a wok, add the eggs and deep-fry about 3–5 minutes, or until golden; remove and drain.

To serve, cover the eggs with the warm sauce and sprinkle with the shallots, garlic, chillies and coriander.

GRILLED DISHES

PORK WITH CHILLI AND LIME JUICE SAUCE

Kor Muu Yang

2 cloves garlic
2 coriander (cilantro) roots
10 white peppercorns
½ teaspoon salt
30 mL (2 tablespoons) sweet soy
    sauce
300 g (10 oz) pork neck (blade)

CHILLI AND LIME JUICE SAUCE
1 teaspoon chilli powder
45 mL (3 tablespoons) fish sauce
90 mL (6 tablespoons) lime juice
4 red shallots, finely sliced
    lengthways
1 teaspoon roasted sticky rice,
    ground (see glossary)
2 tablespoons coriander (cilantro)
    leaves, chopped

THIS IS A simple dish from the north-east of Thailand, where the food is cooked very simply and the flavours are very robust.

If you would prefer a vegetarian dish, substitute whole field mushrooms for the pork. They will only need to be grilled for about 3 minutes.

Method: In a mortar and pestle (or a food processor), crush the garlic, coriander roots, peppercorns and salt until fine, then add the soy sauce. Add the pork to this mixture and marinate overnight.

Grill or broil the pork, turning regularly, for about 10 minutes, or until cooked as desired. Remove and rest for at least 5 minutes. Slice finely and serve with the chilli and lime juice sauce.

To make the chilli and lime juice sauce, combine all of the ingredients in a small bowl. Check that the flavour is hot, sour and salty. Add more chilli powder, lime juice and/or fish sauce as necessary.

CHICKEN WITH SWEET CHILLI SAUCE

Gai Yang Nam Jim Gai Wan

2 coriander (cilantro) roots
5 cloves garlic
15 white peppercorns
1 teaspoon salt
30 mL (2 tablespoons) fish sauce
1 teaspoon palm sugar
1 chicken, about 1 kg (2 lb),
* preferably corn fed*

SWEET CHILLI SAUCE
10 large fresh red chillies, cut in
* half, deseeded and chopped*
1 tablespoon salt
4 coriander (cilantro) roots
6 cloves garlic
250 mL (1 cup/8 fl oz) Thai
* coconut vinegar*
250 g (1 cup/8 oz) white
* (granulated) sugar*

THIS IS THE grilled chicken beloved by all travellers in Thailand. At every bus depot in every village, there is always a person selling it, and it always tastes so good. The trick is to grill the bird slowly and, if possible, over charcoal. The sweet chilli sauce is very easy to make, keeps for several weeks and has a multitude of uses. It goes well with grilled and deep-fried dishes.

Method: In a mortar and pestle (or a food processor), crush the coriander roots, garlic, peppercorns and salt until fine. Cut the chicken in half along the breast bone. Wash, dry and marinate in the paste, fish sauce and palm sugar overnight. Grill or broil slowly over a low heat for about 30 minutes or until cooked. Serve with the sweet chilli sauce.

To make the sweet chilli sauce, in a mortar and pestle (or a food processor), coarsely crush the chillies, salt, coriander roots and garlic. In a small pan combine the paste with vinegar and sugar, and simmer for 10 minutes before serving.

TROUT WITH SWEET FISH SAUCE

Pla Yang Nam Pla Wan

250 g (1 cup/8 oz) palm sugar

100 mL (6½ tablespoons) fish sauce

15 mL (1 tablespoon) tamarind water (see glossary)

1 freshwater trout, about 400 g (14 oz), cleaned and rubbed with salt

5 red shallots, finely sliced lengthways and deep-fried (see glossary)

3 cloves garlic, finely sliced lengthways and deep-fried (see glossary)

6 dried small red chillies, roasted or deep-fried

4 tablespoons coriander (cilantro) leaves, chopped

TRADITIONALLY, THE THAIS would use a freshwater catfish, but I find trout an excellent substitute. If using a charcoal grill, cook the fish over low coals to impart a more smoky flavour. It is often eaten with a bitter vegetable such as *pak sadao*, the neem plant that is occasionally available in Indian food stores. Witlof (chicory or Belgian endive) can take its place.

Method: In a small pan combine the palm sugar, fish sauce and tamarind water, and simmer until the sugar has dissolved, skimming if necessary. It will taste sweet, salty and slightly sour.

Grill or broil the trout until cooked, about 10 minutes over low coals, or about 15 minutes using a conventional grill or broiler.

To serve, place the trout on a serving plate, cover with the warm sauce and sprinkle with the shallots, garlic, chillies and coriander.

SQUID WITH GARLIC AND CHILLI SAUCE

Pla Meuk Pao

*200 g (7 oz) squid or cuttlefish,
   cleaned and skinned*
30 mL (2 tablespoons) soy sauce
*1 teaspoon white (granulated)
   sugar*

GARLIC AND CHILLI SAUCE
*5-10 fresh small red or green
   chillies*
*3 heads pickled garlic (see page
   118), excess skin peeled*
*45 mL (3 tablespoons) pickled
   garlic juice*
1 teaspoon salt
*1 tablespoon white (granulated)
   sugar*

ONE OF THE GREAT joys in Thailand is going to the beaches on the southern peninsula. There, anything — anything — is obtainable, from massages and horseriding to hamburgers and grilled squid.

Method: Marinate the squid in the combined soy sauce and sugar for at least 10 minutes but no longer than 1 hour. Grill or broil for about 5 minutes, or until cooked, and serve with the sauce.

To make the garlic and chilli sauce, in a mortar and pestle (or a food processor), crush together the chillies and pickled garlic. In a small pan simmer the pickled garlic juice with the salt and sugar until the sugar has dissolved. Stir in the paste and simmer for 3-5 minutes. Serve immediately.

KING PRAWNS

Gung Pao

2 cloves garlic
1 coriander (cilantro) root
5 white peppercorns
Pinch salt
Pinch white (granulated) sugar
6 green king prawns (raw jumbo
   shrimp)

SAUCE
1 coriander (cilantro) root
2 cloves garlic (optional)
5-10 fresh small green chillies
Pinch salt
30 mL (2 tablespoons) lime juice
1 teaspoon castor (superfine) sugar
15 mL (1 tablespoon) fish sauce

USE VERY LARGE, fresh prawns or perhaps even a
large mud crab.

Method: In a mortar and pestle (or a food processor),
crush together the garlic, coriander root,
peppercorns, salt and sugar. Marinate the prawns
in this mixture for 1 hour. Grill or broil for about
2 minutes, or until cooked, and serve with the sauce.

To make the sauce, in a mortar and pestle (or a food
processor), crush together the coriander root, garlic,
chillies and salt until fine, then add the lime juice,
sugar and fish sauce to create a hot, sour and
salty taste.

KINGFISH

Pla Samlii Pao

1 clove garlic, crushed with a pinch
　of salt
½ teaspoon ground white pepper
15 mL (1 tablespoon) fish sauce
1 teaspoon white (granulated)
　sugar
30 mL (2 tablespoons) safflower oil
200 g (7 oz) kingfish, hake or
　mullet fillet

SAUCE
60 mL (4 tablespoons) tamarind
　water (see glossary)
2 tablespoons palm sugar
1 teaspoon salt
30 mL (2 tablespoons) fish sauce
5 small dried red chillies, roasted
6 red shallots, sliced lengthways
　and deep-fried (see glossary)

THIS RECIPE IS a generic one for grilling or broiling
fish. Any suitable fish can be used, and any of the
sauces in this section can also be used to accompany
the fish.

Method: Combine the garlic, pepper, fish sauce, sugar
and oil in a bowl. Marinate the fish in this mixture
for 1 hour. Grill or broil the fish for about 8 minutes,
or until cooked, and serve with the sauce.

To make the sauce, in a small pan, simmer together
the tamarind water, sugar and salt for 3 minutes
until quite sticky. Cool and, just before serving, mix
in the fish sauce, chillies and shallots. Serve in a
small bowl.

PERCH WITH CURRY PASTE

Ngob Pla

200 g (7 oz) freshwater perch fillet,
   thinly sliced
3 tablespoons of the curry paste
15 mL (1 tablespoon) fish sauce
1 teaspoon white (granulated)
   sugar
125 mL (½ cup/4 fl oz) coconut
   cream
5 kaffir lime leaves, shredded
2 banana or *cabbage leaves, cut
   into 30 cm (12 in) lengths*

CURRY PASTE
5-20 dried large red chillies,
   deseeded and chopped
6 red shallots, chopped
4 cloves garlic, chopped
1 stalk lemongrass, sliced
1 tablespoon galangal, peeled and
   shredded
1 teaspoon kapi (shrimp paste),
   roasted (see glossary)
1 teaspoon salt

ANY SEAFOOD CAN be used instead of the freshwater perch. It is important to char the banana leaves in order to obtain the smoky flavour which needs to permeate the fish. If using cabbage leaves instead of banana leaves, it is wise not to char them too much as they will impart a bitter flavour to the fish.

Method: In a bowl mix the fish with the curry paste, then add the fish sauce and sugar. Gradually incorporate the coconut cream, then fold in the kaffir lime leaves. Place the mixture in the middle of the banana leaves. Fold the right third over the mixture and then fold the left third over that. Secure the join and ends with toothpicks. Wrap in foil. Grill, broil or roast for 15 minutes, turning regularly. Serve immediately.

To make the curry paste, purée all of the ingredients in a food processor until fine.

RELISHES AND ACCOMPANIMENTS

PRAWN PASTE RELISH

Nam Prik Kapi

3 cloves garlic
Pinch salt
1 tablespoon dried prawns
(shrimp), rinsed
1 tablespoon kapi (shrimp paste),
roasted (see glossary)
5-10 fresh small green chillies
15 mL (1 tablespoon) fish sauce
1 tablespoon palm sugar
30 mL (2 tablespoons) lime juice

EVERY FAMILY HAS a recipe for this particular *Nam Prik*, or relish. Its flavours, textures and ingredients are elemental and its taste is quintessentially Thai. There is an interplay of sour, salty and hot and the pungency of roasted kapi that is excellent eaten with crisp raw vegetables such as cucumbers and green beans. There are myriad variations on this *Nam Prik* — you can add grilled prawns or finely shredded green mango, for example. Thai food is very adaptable and new dishes are made by the judicious addition of new ingredients.

Method: In a mortar and pestle, combine the garlic, salt and prawns, and pound until quite fine. Add the kapi and chillies and pound lightly until mixed together, moistening with a little warm water. Add the fish sauce, palm sugar and lime juice. Stir and serve. The number of chillies you use will, of course, affect how hot the *Nam Prik* will be. So will the degree to which you pound them: if you want the taste and fragrance of the chillies, then do not pound them too much — indeed, just crush them lightly, or add some of them after adding the lime juice.

RELISH OF SALTY DUCK EGGS WITH FRESH VEGETABLES

Nam Prik Kai Kem

3 cloves garlic
Pinch salt
6 small fresh green chillies
1 teaspoon kapi (shrimp paste),
   roasted (see glossary)
2 tablespoons dried prawns
   (shrimp)
2 salty duck eggs (see page 116),
   hardboiled and peeled
½ head pickled garlic (see page
   118), sliced (optional)
6-8 pea eggplants (aubergines),
   crushed
1 teaspoon tamarind water (see
   glossary)
1 teaspoon palm sugar
15 mL (1 tablespoon) lime juice
30 mL (2 tablespoons) water

THIS IS MY FAVOURITE *Nam Prik* — the saltiness of the duck eggs marries well with the heat of the chillies and the sourness of the lime juice. It is good eaten with lots of *Yam Pla Fuu* (Crispy Fish Salad, see page 35) and *Muu Wan* (Sweet Pork, see page 120) and fresh vegetables such as savoy cabbage, cucumber and green beans.

Method: In a mortar and pestle, pound the garlic and salt until fine, then add the chillies, kapi and prawns. Crush until well mixed. Crumble in the eggs, mix in the pickled garlic and eggplants, then add the tamarind water, palm sugar, lime juice and water. Just before serving, check the taste. It should be pungently salty, and a little sour and sweet. Adjust, if necessary, by adding more tamarind water, lime juice and/or palm sugar. The heat from the chillies should be just enough to balance the salt from the eggs, no more — unless, of course, you are a masochist.

NORTHERN CHILLI RELISH

Nam Prik Nuum

4 banana chillies, roasted, skinned and deseeded

5 red shallots, roasted and peeled (see glossary)

2 cloves garlic, roasted and peeled (see glossary)

3 cherry (baby) tomatoes, grilled (broiled)

1 teaspoon salt

1 teaspoon white (granulated) sugar

45 mL (3 tablespoons) nam pla ra (see glossary)

KHUN PEN IS a very well-known chef in Chiang Mai. When I first met her at her restaurant, Heun Pen, she was delightful, and her food even more so. Indeed, I have never, as yet, come across a restaurant in Thailand where there was so much care taken with the food. In a home, yes, but so far never in a restaurant. Here, then, is her recipe for a classic northern relish, which should be eaten with some *Muu Grop* (Crispy Fried Pork, see page 97) and a poached freshwater fish.

Method: In a mortar and pestle pound all the ingredients except the *nam pla ra* until well mixed. Stir in the *nam pla ra* to create a flavour that is predominantly smoky, not too hot — as northern food rarely is — and fragrant from the charring and the *nam pla ra*. Serve in a small bowl.

RELISH OF CRAB WITH FRESH TAMARIND

Nam Prik Makam Sot Gap Bpu

1 teaspoon salt

3 cloves garlic

3-5 small fresh green chillies

1 teaspoon kapi (shrimp paste),
   roasted (see glossary)

1 tablespoon dried prawns
   (shrimp)

3 tamarind pods

15 mL (1 tablespoon) safflower oil

50 g (2 oz) pork, minced (ground)

15 mL (1 tablespoon) tamarind
   paste

100 g (4 oz) crab meat

15 mL (1 tablespoon) fish sauce

1 teaspoon palm sugar

15 mL (1 tablespoon) tamarind
   water (see glossary) or lime juice

THIS IS A TART relish that is served warm. It should be eaten with vegetables, *Kai Kem* (Salty Eggs, see page 116) and perhaps *Muu Wan* (Sweet Pork, see page 120). Prawns may be used instead of crab meat.

Method: In a mortar and pestle, pound the salt, garlic, chillies, kapi, prawns and fresh tamarind until fine.

In a small pan heat the oil, add the pork and fry about 3 minutes or until cooked. Add the tamarind paste and fry until fragrant. Take off the heat and mix in the crab, fish sauce, palm sugar and tamarind water or lime juice. It will taste very pungent and very hot as well as sour and salty. The Thais often add a few more fresh chillies to the paste and some lightly crushed pickled pea eggplants (aubergines) before serving.

MINCED PRAWNS IN COCONUT CREAM

Lon Gung

375 mL (1½ cups/12 fl oz) coconut
   cream
Pinch salt
5 large green prawns (raw shrimp),
   finely chopped
2 tablespoons white (granulated)
   sugar
30 mL (2 tablespoons) tamarind
   water (see glossary)
15 mL (1 tablespoon) fish sauce
½ small green mango, julienned
4 red shallots, sliced lengthways
2-5 large fresh red or green
   chillies, cut into 1 cm (⅓ in)
   lengths
2 tablespoons fresh coriander
   (cilantro) leaves

FROM AN ANTHOLOGY of recipes published in 1926, this particular *lon* is ascribed to Mom Luang Yingdin Clamarakpitjan. It is elegant and easy to make. It is served with either a grilled, broiled or deep-fried freshwater fish, and of course fresh vegetables, especially savoy cabbage. It is also delicious with steamed prawns.

Method: In a medium pan bring the coconut cream and salt to the boil, add the prawns and cook for about 3 minutes, stirring constantly to prevent the prawns from clumping. When they are cooked and the mixture is rather thick, add the sugar, tamarind water, fish sauce, mango, shallots and chillies. Sprinkle with the coriander leaves and serve.

The finished taste should be rather creamy, slightly sour, salty and a little sweet. Add more tamarind water, fish sauce and sugar if necessary.

YELLOW BEANS IN COCONUT CREAM

Lon Tow Jiaw

*3-5 large dried red chillies,
   deseeded and sliced*

7 red shallots

*125 mL (½ cup/4 fl oz) Thai
   yellow bean sauce, strained and
   beans washed to remove some of
   the saltiness*

*250 mL (1 cup/8 fl oz) coconut
   cream*

*100 g (4 oz) prawns (shrimp),
   finely chopped (optional)*

*100 g (4 oz) pork, minced (ground)
   (optional)*

*250 mL (1 cup/8 fl oz) coconut
   milk*

*45 mL (3 tablespoons) tamarind
   water (see glossary)*

45 mL (3 tablespoons) palm sugar

*2 fresh long red or green chillies,
   sliced into 1 cm (⅓ in) lengths*

*2 tablespoons fresh coriander
   (cilantro) leaves*

THIS IS A RECIPE from Khun Yai, the woman who first showed me the intricacies of Thai food. In this Thai *lon* there is no need for fish sauce or salt as the yellow beans are quite salty. This lends well to making it a vegetarian accompaniment, as the prawns and pork may be omitted.

As with all *lons*, this one is served with fresh vegetables. It also combines nicely with freshly steamed king prawns (jumbo shrimp) and a very hot dish, such as *Pat Prik King Tua Fak Yaew* (Pork with Snake Beans and Chilli Paste, see page 87).

Method: Pound or blend the dried chillies, 4 of the shallots and yellow beans. In a medium pan heat the coconut cream, then add the pounded paste and cook for about 5 minutes or until fragrant, stirring regularly. Mix in the prawn and pork, if using, and cook for about 10 minutes, stirring constantly to prevent the meat from clumping. Add coconut milk and simmer until thick, about 3 minutes. When cooked add the tamarind water and palm sugar. Finely slice lengthways 3 remaining shallots.

To serve, garnish with the fresh chillies, sliced shallots and coriander leaves. It should taste sweet, salty and sour. Add more palm sugar and/or tamarind water if necessary.

KAPI PASTE SIMMERED IN COCONUT CREAM

Lon Kapi

*500 mL (2 cups/16 fl oz) coconut
cream*
All of the kapi (shrimp) paste
2-3 tablespoons palm sugar
15 mL (1 tablespoon) fish sauce
*250 mL (1 cup/8 fl oz) coconut
milk*
Fresh long red chillies, sliced

KAPI (SHRIMP) PASTE
*6 large dried red chillies, deseeded
and chopped*
1 stalk lemongrass, sliced
*1 tablespoon peeled and chopped
galangal*
8 stalks krachai (see glossary)
6 red shallots, sliced
4 cloves garlic
*2 tablespoons kapi (shrimp paste),
roasted (see glossary)*
*3 tablespoons dried prawns
(shrimp) or pla grop (see
glossary)*
1 teaspoon salt

THIS *LON* SHOULD be served with some fresh vegetables such as savoy cabbage, cucumbers, green mango and, if possible, white turmeric. It is also delicious with crisp fried fish.

Method: In a medium pan bring the coconut cream to the boil. When it has separated, about 8–10 minutes, add the kapi paste and cook over a low heat, stirring regularly, for about 10 minutes or until the paste is fragrant. Add the palm sugar, fish sauce and coconut milk. Continue to cook over a low heat until the *lon* has reached a thick consistency, about 10 minutes. Check that the flavour is creamy, salty and slightly sweet. Add more fish sauce and/or palm sugar if necessary.

To serve, garnish with the sliced chillies.

To make the kapi paste, mix all of the ingredients in a food processor, using as little water as possible, until fine.

SALTY EGGS

Kai Kem

200 g (7 oz) salt
2 L (8 cups/3½ pt) water
12 duck eggs or 18 chicken eggs

SALTING EGGS WAS the method used by the Thais to preserve eggs before the advent of refrigeration. It radically changes the taste and texture of the egg: the raw yolks, for example, become almost as hard as if they had been cooked. They are certainly an acquired taste but, once acquired, addictive. The saltiness is used to enhance the creaminess and heat of curries.

Method: In a large pan combine the salt and water, and bring to the boil to make a brine. Cool, and immerse the eggs for at least a month. Store in an airtight plastic container in the refrigerator.

These eggs can be served either boiled or deep-fried. To deep-fry, allow one uncooked egg per person. Separate each yolk and whisk each egg white separately until stiff. Into four beaten egg whites, fold 1 teaspoon of rice flour, and 1 chopped egg yolk, then deep-fry in spoonfuls until golden.

SALTY BEEF

Neua Kem

500 g (1 lb) beef (any cut will do)
3 tablespoons salt
45 mL (3 tablespoons) fish sauce
1 tablespoon palm sugar
10 white peppercorns, ground
1 L (4 cups/1¾ pt) safflower oil for
   deep-frying

THIS ACCOMPANIMENT IS wonderful with a green or sour orange curry. It is also very good when, after preparing it according to this recipe, it is simmered in coconut milk until tender and then served sprinkled with sliced red shallots, finely sliced lemongrass and chillies. When Thais go on long journeys they often carry some of this dried beef, tossed in sugar and spices, to snack on.

Method: Slice the beef along the grain into ½ cm (¼ in) slices. Combine the beef with the salt, fish sauce, palm sugar and pepper, and marinate for 3 hours. Lay the slices out on a tray, making sure they do not overlap, and dry out in a low oven for 4 hours. When dry, store in an airtight container in the refrigerator. It will keep for about 1 month.

To serve, rehydrate the beef in water for 20 minutes. In a wok, deep-fry the beef for 2 minutes over a medium heat, remove, drain and pound the meat in a mortar and pestle or with a mallet to break the fibres. Refry the meat for another minute, then drain and again pound the meat. Allow the meat to cool, then shred finely.

To make sweet salty beef, in a wok heat 15 mL (1 tablespoon) safflower oil and add 3 tablespoons palm sugar. Stir until it begins to caramelise, about 3 minutes, then incorporate 150 g (5 oz) salty beef and 15 mL (1 tablespoon) fish sauce. Cool, then mix in 4 deep-fried shallots (see glossary). Serve sprinkled with chopped raw shallots and coriander (cilantro) leaves.

PICKLED GARLIC

Gratiam Dong

200 g (7 oz) garlic cloves
250 g (1 cup/8 oz) white
  (granulated) sugar
185 mL (¾ cup/6 fl oz) Thai
  coconut vinegar
1 tablespoon salt
250 mL (1 cup/8 fl oz) water

PICKLED GARLIC IS wonderful when eaten with
a jungle curry or stir-fried with eggs and pork.
It provides a good balance for any dish that is
very hot, sour or salty.

Method: Peel the garlic, soak in salted water
overnight, then rinse. In a medium pan, combine
the sugar, vinegar, salt and water. Bring to the boil,
stirring, and when the sugar has dissolved, remove
from the heat and cool. Place the garlic into a
resealable bottle and cover with the liquid.
Store in an airtight container in the refrigerator
for 1 month before using.

PICKLED VEGETABLES
Pak Dong

100 g (1 cup/4 oz) diced cucumber
100 g (1 cup/4 oz) cauliflower
   florets
100 g (1 cup/4 oz) shredded
   cabbage
100 g (1 cup/4 oz) baby corn
500 mL (2 cups/16 fl oz) Thai
   coconut vinegar
3 cloves garlic, chopped
2 long fresh red chillies, deseeded
   and chopped
3 red shallots, chopped
1 teaspoon salt
45 mL (3 tablespoons) safflower oil

THIS PICKLE IS a good accompaniment to a thick red curry, its acid and sugar providing a pleasant foil for the richness of the coconut cream. This pickle can be prepared a few days ahead and can be made with most vegetables. It is especially good when shallots are included, as here.

Method: Blanch all the vegetables in the vinegar. In a mortar and pestle (or a food processor), crush the garlic, chillies, shallots and salt until fine. Fry this paste in the oil until fragrant. Add the blanched vegetables and vinegar and simmer for a few minutes. Cool before serving.

SWEET PORK

Muu Wan

300 g (10 oz) pork neck (blade)
125 g (½ cup/4 oz) white (granulated) sugar
15 mL (1 tablespoon) water
30 mL (2 tablespoons) fish sauce
15 mL (1 tablespoon) dark soy sauce
30 mL (2 tablespoons) extra water
10 red shallots, sliced and deep-fried until golden (see glossary, optional)

THIS IS ADDICTIVE. It is quite possible that the quantities given here will only be enough for one person. It is eaten as an accompaniment to *Nam Priks* (relishes). The sugar mitigates the heat from the chillies. I think it should be on the table regardless of what else is there, for the sheer indulgence of it.

Method: Steam the pork until cooked, then cut into ½ cm (¼ in) cubes. In a small pan combine the sugar and water, and cook until it caramelises. Add the pork, fish sauce, soy sauce and extra water. Simmer for 5 minutes until sticky. Mix in the deep-fried shallots and serve.

DESSERTS

DESSERTS

A REGULAR THAI MEAL is usually completed with a platter of fresh tropical fruit: pawpaws (papayas), mangoes and pineapples, which may be enhanced by a squeeze of lime juice and a sprinkle of salt. At a formal meal, two different styles of dessert may be offered: wet, such as Banana Stewed in Coconut Milk, and dry, such as Crisp Pancakes.

Normally, however, what we would call desserts are eaten in between meals — as snacks. Beside the vendor of savoury snacks there is invariably a dessert stall where sweetmeats are purveyed. This is why some desserts are quite rich and filling, because they are meant to sustain between meals, not to complete them.

The Thais take great pride in their desserts, believing them to be a high point in their cuisine. The techniques required are often more intricate than those used in savoury food. The brown skin of the husked coconut meat is removed to ensure a gleamingly white cream, jasmine flowers are steeped in water to instil their perfume, and sugar syrups are clarified with egg white to improve their sheen. These are just a few of the Thai confectioner's skills.

BANANA STEWED IN COCONUT MILK

Gluay Buat Chii

250 mL (1 cup/8 fl oz) coconut
   milk
5 bananas, just ripe, cut into 5 cm
   (2 in) lengths
200 g (7 oz) white (granulated)
   sugar
1 teaspoon salt
250 mL (1 cup/8 fl oz) coconut
   cream

ANY FIRM TROPICAL fruit or even sliced pumpkin (squash) may be used in this recipe. The Thais enjoy a salty bite in some of their desserts. However, this can be alarming to Westerners, so omit the salt, if desired.

Method: In a small enamel or glass (stainless steel may discolour the milk) pan, bring the coconut milk to the boil. Add the bananas and simmer for about 5 minutes, or until cooked. Add the sugar and salt and stir to dissolve. Stir in the coconut cream and serve.

COCONUT CUSTARD IN PUMPKIN

Sangkaya Fak Thong

*250 mL (1 cup/8 fl oz) coconut
    cream*
*100 g (½ cup/4 oz) white
    (granulated) sugar*
2 pandanus leaves (optional)
2 eggs
Pinch salt
*1 teaspoon rice flour or cornflour
    (cornstarch)*
*1 pumpkin (squash) weighing
    about 1 kg (2 lb)*

A CLASSIC THAI dessert that is eaten on the street and at home, it is often garnished with *Foi Tong* (Golden Egg Threads, see page 132). Do not steam over too fierce a heat as this may cause the custard to curdle.

Method: In either an enamel or glass bowl (stainless steel may discolour the coconut cream), combine the coconut cream, sugar, pandanus leaves, eggs, salt and flour. Stir for 5 minutes to dissolve the sugar and infuse the cream with the pandanas leaves.

Slice the top off the pumpkin and scoop out the seeds. Strain the mixture into the pumpkin and steam over a medium heat for 45 minutes, or until the pumpkin is tender and the custard mixture is firm. Allow to cool, preferably overnight, to settle before serving. Slice in wedges and serve.

DEEP-FRIED BANANAS

Gluay Kaek Tort

100 g (1 cup/4 oz) rice flour
Pinch salt
100 g (4 oz) fresh coconut, grated
50 g (2 oz) white (granulated)
*   sugar*
1 tablespoon sesame seeds
125 mL (½ cup/4 fl oz) water
5 sugar or ladies fingers (small
*   sweet) bananas, peeled*
1 L (4 cups/1¾ pt) safflower oil for
*   deep-frying*

IN ALL THE MARKETS throughout Thailand, there are huge woks filled with boiling oil that are used to deep-fry bananas. Perhaps the most delicious part of the dessert is the batter — some Thais buy this just for the fried batter! Indulgent but delicious.

Method: Sift the flour with the salt into a bowl. Stir in the coconut, sugar and sesame seeds and whisk in the water. Allow to stand for 5 minutes. The batter should coat the bananas easily. If it is too thick add another 30 mL (2 tablespoons) of water.

Slice the bananas lengthways, dip into the batter and deep-fry, a few slices at a time, in a wok half-filled with oil over a medium heat. Remove, drain and serve immediately.

STICKY RICE WITH MANGO

Kaow Niaw Mamuang

500 g (2 cups/1 lb) sticky rice
750 mL (3 cups/1¼ pt) coconut
*   cream*
1 pandanus leaf (see glossary)
350 g (1½ cups/12 oz) white
*   (granulated) sugar*
Pinch salt
3 medium mangoes, sliced
Fresh coconut cream

THE THAIS LOOK forward to the mango season so that they can devour this dessert. However, there is no reason to wait for mangoes: custard apples, jackfruits, lychees, bananas and even poached pears can be used.

Method: Cover the sticky rice with water and leave to swell overnight. Rinse the sticky rice in several changes of water, then steam for 20 minutes, or until the grains are tender. Meanwhile, in an enamel or glass bowl (stainless steel may discolour the coconut cream) combine the coconut cream, pandanus leaf, white sugar and salt. Stir for about 10 minutes, or until the sugar has dissolved. When the rice is cooked, turn it into a bowl and then pour over the coconut cream mixture. Cover the bowl and allow the grains to absorb the cream in a warm place for at least 10 minutes, but no longer than 3 hours. Serve with the mangoes and fresh coconut cream.

STICKY PUDDING

Kanom Nam Tan

100 g (1 cup/4 oz) rice flour
2 tablespoons tapioca flour
1 teaspoon salt
500 mL (2 cups/16 fl oz) coconut
    cream
500 g (2 cups/1 lb) palm sugar
2 pandanus leaves (see glossary,
    optional)
100 g (1 cup/4 oz) freshly grated
    coconut
125 mL (½ cup/4 fl oz) coconut
    cream

A VERY FILLING DESSERT, this is typical of the sweet snacks available from the street hawkers that abound in Thailand. Should the mixture clump while cooking, just remove the pandanus leaves, whirl the mixture in the food processor and then return to the pot with the pandanus leaves.

Method: Sieve the flours and salt into a bowl, then whisk in the cream and sugar. Strain into a medium pot and add the pandanus leaves. Cook over a medium heat, stirring constantly to prevent the mixture from sticking, for 15-20 minutes, or until the taste is neither floury nor grainy. Pour the mixture into a tray, smooth it out and allow to cool.

Cut into 1.5 cm (½ in) cubes and serve either by itself or rolled in some freshly grated coconut and coconut cream.

TAPIOCA PUDDING

Kanom Saku

100 g (1 cup/4 oz) tapioca flour
2 tablespoons sticky rice flour
50 g (½ cup/2 oz) rice flour
Pinch salt
500 mL (1 cup/8 fl oz) coconut
    water (see glossary)
500 g (2 cups/1 lb) white
    (granulated) sugar
250 mL (½ cup/4 fl oz) extra
    coconut water, puréed with 4
    pandanus leaves (see glossary)
    and strained
Fresh coconut cream

THIS RECIPE IS far removed from the heaviness of Western-style tapioca puddings. It is a very sweet dessert, and often it is improved with the addition of lychees or young coconut meat, in the final stages of cooking.

Method: Soak the tapioca in warm water for 1 hour so the grains can swell. In a small pan combine the flours with the salt and 500 mL (1 cup/8 fl oz) coconut water and cook over a medium heat, stirring constantly, until it is sticky and beginning to turn opaque, about 5 minutes. Strain the tapioca, add to the pan and continue to cook for about 10 minutes or until the tapioca has turned transparent. Taste to check that the flours are also cooked, it will be smooth and not floury. Stir in the sugar until it has dissolved, then add the pandanus water. Continue to cook for a further 2–3 minutes until the herbaceous aroma from the raw pandanus has disappeared. Remove from the heat and allow to cool. Serve in bowls with fresh coconut cream.

GOLDEN EGG THREADS

Foi Tong

5 duck eggs
5 chicken eggs (or 12, if duck eggs
   unobtainable)
500 g (2 cups/1 lb) castor
   (superfine) sugar
500 mL (2 cups/16 fl oz) water

THIS DESSERT WAS introduced to the Thais by the Portuguese in the sixteenth century. Although the recipe seems simple it is deceptive — only with practice is success assured. If the noodles crinkle while boiling, the syrup is too heavy. Dilute it with an extra 2 tablespoons of water. Alternatively, if they are too watery, remove the noodles, strain the liquid, return to the pan and boil for a minute to make a denser syrup.

These noodles go well with *Sangkaya Fak Thong* (Coconut Custard in Pumpkin, see page 127) and *Kanom Beaung* (Crisp Pancakes, see page 133).

Method: Separate the eggs, combining any of the thick albumen still attached to the shell with the egg yokes. Strain this through a very fine sieve. Use the egg whites for another dish.

In a low, wide pan, bring the sugar and water to the boil. When the sugar has dissolved, turn down the heat.

Pour the egg yolks into a piping bag fitted with a very, very fine nozzle. Stream this mixture backward and forward into the boiling syrup. Do not overcrowd the pan with the noodles as they will clump and cook unevenly. When they have cooked for 3 minutes, remove from the pan with chopsticks or a fork. Lay out the threads, then fold them into thirds. Replenish the pot with about 30–45 mL (2–3 tablespoons) of water to compensate for evaporation. Bring back to the boil and repeat this process until all the mixture is used. Allow the noodles to dry. Traditionally, the threads are stored in an airtight container overnight with some freshly picked Thai jasmine flowers.

CRISP PANCAKES

Kanom Beaung

2 tablespoons mung bean flour
2 tablespoons rice flour
2 tablespoons plain (all-purpose)
  flour
1 tablespoon arrowroot
Salt
½ small egg white, lightly beaten
125 mL (½ cup/4 fl oz) water

FILLING
200 g (2 cups/7 oz) freshly grated
  coconut
50 g (2 oz) sliced dried persimmon
50 g (2 oz) Golden Egg Threads
  (see page 132)
1 teaspoon sesame seeds, roasted

PROBABLY ONE OF the most elegant of Thai desserts, *Kanom Beaung* can be filled with various ingredients, such as *Foi Tong* (Golden Egg Threads, see page 132), candied fruit or even dried prawns.

Method: Sift the flours, arrowroot and salt together. Add the egg white and water and mix well until a smooth batter is achieved. Rest for 1 hour before use.

Spoon 1 tablespoon of the batter onto a warm non-stick frying pan and smooth out into an oval or round shape. Cook over a medium heat until it begins to turn golden. Lift off the pancake with a spatula and while it is still warm and flexible, curl over a spoon. Once it is cool it becomes brittle. To serve, fill with the grated coconut, persimmon, Golden Egg Noodles and sesame seeds.

GLOSSARY

AUBERGINE (see Eggplant)

BAMBOO/NOR MAI Fresh bamboo is not readily obtainable in the West, but if it can be found, do use it as it has quite a different taste to canned bamboo. To prepare fresh bamboo, peel and finely slice the bamboo stalk; wash it and then blanch it in boiling salted water; drain and refresh. Bring some fresh salted water to the boil, then add the blanched bamboo and simmer for about 10 minutes, or until tender and not too bitter. To prepare canned bamboo (either whole or sliced), rinse it in several changes of water, then place in enough cold salted water to cover, bring to a boil, boil for 1 minute, then drain under cold running water.

BANANA BLOSSOMS/HUA BPLII These are the buds of the banana tree. They are a rusty purple in colour and should be firm to the touch when purchasing. Open out one or two of the sheaths, and if the insides of the sheaths are not creamy or are going black do not buy, as they will at best be tasteless or, worse, very bitter. To prepare banana blossoms, remove the outer sheaths to reveal the white heart. Quarter the heart, remove the core and stamens, and finely slice the quarters on a bias. Immerse in acidulated water (water with 45 mL/3 tablespoons vinegar, lime juice or lemon juice added) to prevent discolouring. Try not to clean the banana blossoms more than 30 minutes before use as they will darken. The stamens should be removed as they are very bitter and the sheaths should be sliced very finely before using. If banana blossoms are not available, artichokes are a possible substitute.

BANANA LEAVES/BAI TONG Always wash before use. If they are particularly unmanageable, immerse in hot water to soften them.

BANANAS/GLUAY The Thais produce several varieties of banana, of which the sugar banana (*Gluay Nam Wai*) is the most popular. If sugar bananas are not available, substitute ordinary bananas. When deep-frying, use plantains.

BASIL The Thais use three types of basil. First and most important is Thai basil, **Bai Horapha**, a pungently anise basil, similar in appearance to sweet basil. It is used in red and green curries. Sweet basil may be substituted. Secondly, there is holy or hot basil, **Bai Grapao**, a herb redolent of cloves, which should be bought on the day of use. Finally, there is **Bai Manglaek**, a lemon basil used in soups.

BAY LEAF/BAI GRAWAN This leaf is used in Massaman Curry and occasionally with beef soups. Although the Western bay leaf is not related, it has a similar taste and is a very satisfactory substitute.

BEANCURD/TOR HUU Also called tofu, it is the preferred vegetarian substitute for meat. It is made from soy beans and is low in carbohydrates but rich in protein. It is readily available. Upon opening, beancurd should be rinsed, then kept in water that is changed daily and stored in the refrigerator. It will keep for 5 days.

BETEL LEAVES/BAI CHAMPLUU These are closely related to the betel nut, although they do not have the same effect. This leaf has a slightly acidic orange flavour and is dark green in colour. If it is not available, young spinach, butter lettuce or coral lettuce may be used as an alternative.

BITTER MELONS/MARA The Thais, like the Chinese, believe that this melon is very good for the blood and kidneys. Always buy small, firm melons that are light green in colour. Before cooking, the melon needs to be cut in half and the seeds removed. Most authorities suggest that a single blanching is necessary before using. I prefer to salt it for 30 minutes to help leach out the bitterness, then blanch from a cold water start.

CARDAMOM/LUK GRAWAN Although not common to Thai cooking, cardamom sometimes appears in dishes that have been adapted from other cuisines, such as Massaman Curry. Use the small off-white pod whole, and discard before serving. Normal (green Indian) cardamom can be used, but as it is much more pungent, reduce the quantity by half.

CASSIA BARK/OB CHOEY This spice is readily obtainable in Chinese food stores. It is related to cinnamon, which can be substituted, however, the flavour of cassia is richer and oilier and its quills are much larger and coarser. Like cardamom, it is normally used in adapted dishes, such as Massaman Curry.

CELERY/KEUN CHAI Asian celery looks very much like Italian parsley. It is more pungent than Western celery, but easily interchangeable.

CHILLIES/PRIK It is hard to believe that chillies only reached Thailand in the sixteenth century via the Portuguese, so integral are they to the cuisine. The Thais use many varieties of chilli, the most memorable being the bird's eye chilli, **Prik Kii Noo Suan**, a small, thin, green or occasionally red chilli. It is viciously hot, yet has such a wonderfully floral aftertaste that, once accustomed to its heat, one cannot do without its flavour. Search it out in Asian providores. Any other hot chilli can be substituted, although nothing else will produce quite the same depth of flavour. These chillies are also available dried and are readily obtainable in Asian food shops. Dried, they are used in making curry pastes, especially for southern curries. Long chillies, **Prik Chii Fa**, are about 5 cm (2 in) long and may be red, green or yellow. They are used as a garnish in curries and salads, and the dried form is the one most often used in red curries. When buying, always look for the darkest coloured ones.

To make chillies with vinegar, place 15 fresh large red chillies in a bowl, then cover with Thai coconut vinegar.

To make roasted chilli powder, deseed and wash the dried chillies. In a wok or pan, dry roast them over a moderate heat until they are slightly darker and fragrant. Do not let them burn. Remove from heat and grind in a mortar and pestle until fine.

CILANTRO (see Coriander)

COCONUT/MAPRAO When buying a coconut always choose one that seems quite heavy for its size, this means that there will be more meat, so it should yield more cream. Shake the nut to ensure that it is full of water — this water is rarely used in cooking. If there is no water, do not buy as it quite probably will be fermented.

The taste of fresh coconut cream is incomparable. It is rich and has a complexity and depth of flavour that justifies the task of making your own. To make coconut cream, crack open the coconut over a bowl, then grate the meat with a Thai coconut grater, called a rabbit. This grater has very sharp prongs that ensure a finely grated coconut. The grated meat should be covered with hot water and left to soak for 10 minutes. When the water has cooled, squeeze the juice from the meat into another bowl, strain and stand for 30 minutes to allow the cream to rise to the top. To make coconut milk, repeat this process using more warm water. The coconut cream is made from the first pressing and the milk is the product of the second pressing.

The cream should be refrigerated and used within two days, otherwise it begins to ferment. Should it begin to sour, arrest the fermentation by bringing the cream and the milk to the boil and simmering it slowly, stirring occasionally for 5 minutes. So treated the cream and milk will last for a week. However it is not as luscious as fresh, unboiled cream and this method should only be used to save the cream.

One coconut normally yields around 250 mL (1 cup/8 fl oz) cream and the amount of milk is determined by the amount of water used to squeeze the cream and the milk.

Roasted coconut is grated coconut that has been dry fried in a wok over a very low heat, for 5–10 minutes, or until golden, turning the meat constantly to ensure that it does not scorch.

For separating the cream, see Curries.

CORIANDER (CILANTRO)/PAK CHII Thais use all of the coriander plant, including the roots, which should be scraped before using. They impart a stronger flavour, but if the herb comes without roots, the stems may be used.

CORIANDER (CILANTRO) SEED/LUUK PAK CHII Thai coriander seed is much smaller and a lot sharper in flavour than the Western variety, which can be substituted. It is easily obtainable from any Asian food store.

To roast coriander seed, dry roast in a pan over a low heat, tossing regularly to prevent the spices from scorching. Do not cook for too long, the colour should only slightly darken.

CUCUMBERS/TAENG GWA Thai cucumbers are much smaller than those available in the West, however, there is little appreciable difference when they are cut up. Lebanese cucumbers make a good substitute. To roll cut, after washing the vegetable, top and tail it, then slice it at a 45° angle, turn slightly and slice again at a 45° angle.

CUMIN SEED/YIIRA Thai cumin seed is similar to the Western variety, which may be substituted. It is always used with coriander (cilantro) seed, usually in the proportion of 2 coriander seeds : 1 cumin. Cumin seeds should be dry roasted very slowly to prevent scorching. They are ready when they are slightly darker in colour and are fragrant.

CURRIES/GAENG Thai curries have a profuse range of flavours and the only way to ensure true reproduction of these flavours is by making the curry paste yourself. It should take no more than 30 minutes to prepare and the result is, without doubt, worth the extra time involved. The recipes for the curry pastes will often yield more than is required. The pastes should last 2 weeks if stored in an airtight container in the refrigerator.

Always chop the ingredients required for the curry paste as finely as possible before processing to a fine purée. It is crucial that the paste be puréed as finely as possible so that when it is cooked and moistened with liquid, it can dissolve completely, leaving no trace of the fibrous nature of the ingredients used. A food processor is the best equipment for reducing the paste to a pulp. Purists would insist that a mortar and pestle is the only way to make a paste, but it is a daunting and exhausting task which will only deter rather than encourage. The paste may need to be moistened with a little water to facilitate blending, but use only the minimum amount necessary.

When cooking the curry paste in coconut cream, the coconut cream needs to be boiled until the water has evaporated and the cream has separated or cracked and is oily. This enables the curry to be cooked at the high temperatures required. When separating the cream, stir constantly, as the sugars in the cream tend to caramelise and catch on the sides of the pan, giving a scorched rather than a nutty flavour. If canned rather than fresh coconut cream is being used, do not shake the can before opening — simply lift off the solid plug of coconut cream at the top which then can be used following the recipe. Often, canned coconut cream is heavily processed and so stabilised that it is difficult to separate (and often has a gluey, gluggy taste). To avoid this, boil the coconut cream until it has reduced by one-third. If it still shows no sign of separating, add 1–2 tablespoons of safflower oil to the liquid, allow it to boil for 1 minute, and then add the curry paste.

Cook the paste over a constantly medium flame, stirring to prevent it from catching and to ensure even cooking — should the paste be a little too dry, moisten with some more coconut cream. The frying time can alter considerably, so use the time given in the recipes as a guide, not gospel. As the paste continues to cook, its character begins to change — the colour deepens and as the water evaporates, the paste becomes less pulpy. More importantly, the aroma changes: the citrus perfume dissipates on heating and as the ingredients begin to cook at different temperatures, so at first there is an aroma of garlic and shallots, then lemongrass and galangal, and so on until, finally, you can smell the dried spices. As the flavours deepen and mellow, you should judge whether the paste is cooked by your eyes, nose and tongue, not by the clock. It should smell cooked and the paste should be marbled and sizzling in the coconut cream, as most of the water from the paste has by now evaporated.

Season the paste with the fish sauce and palm sugar, and continue to fry for a further minute so that the fish sauce has cooked and the sugar has bonded with the paste. Stir to assist this. Moisten with the coconut milk and complete the recipe. All fried curries are treated in much the same manner, although curries that use fresh green chillies as their base should be cooked over a high heat for only 3–5 minutes to ensure that the sharp, fresh flavour of the chillies is not lost. The rich, thick red curries that use dried red chillies as their base should be cooked for at least 5–8 minutes, until the fragrance is mellow, nutty and redolent of spices.

The boiled curries, such as the Sour Orange Curry, are much simpler curries, relying on only a few ingredients. They do not require prolonged cooking or complicated techniques. Although they are simple, they are nonetheless satisfying.

CURRY POWDER/PONG GARI There are many commercially made curry powders available and if their quality and freshness are assured, then use them without hesitation. But if uncertain, here is a recipe that can be used whenever curry powder is called for. Grind together until very fine 2 teaspoons of the following: chilli powder, ground turmeric, roasted cumin seed, powdered ginger, black peppercorns, roasted cardamom pods; 1 teaspoon each of roasted coriander (cilantro) seed, roasted mace and fennel seeds; 5 roasted cloves; 1 nutmeg; and a 2 cm (¾ in) piece of roasted cassia bark. Store the powder in an airtight container in the refrigerator. Should the powder be a little stale, roast it very lightly in a skillet over medium heat for 1 minute to revive its fragrance.

DRIED PRAWNS (SHRIMP)/GUNG HAENG This is one of the few instances where store-bought is better and these are readily available in Asian markets. Always buy the prawns (shrimp) that have the deepest red colour and smell the sweetest. Store them in the refrigerator as they do deteriorate.

EGGPLANTS (AUBERGINES) It is believed that eggplants (aubergines) originated in Thailand and the cuisine enjoys several varieties. Long eggplants, **Makreua Yaew**, look and taste very similar to long baby (Japanese) eggplants, which can be substituted, except that they are green in colour. These eggplants are normally served simply grilled or broiled or in green curries. Apple eggplants, **Makreua Prao**, are green, yellow-orange or purple in colour and round in shape. They are normally eaten raw or barely cooked in salads, curries or as a vegetable on a *nam prik* or *lon* plate. They discolour rapidly, so if you're slicing them in advance, store them in salted water. Pea eggplants, **Makreua Puang**, are pea-sized berries which grow in clusters. Although somewhat bitter, their taste is a pleasant foil against the richness of the curries in which they are most often found. Hairy eggplants, **Maeuk**, an uncommon variety, are round and 1 cm (½ in) in diameter and surprisingly sour. They need to be scraped before using. Substitute with Western or Japanese eggplant if none of these varieties is available.

FISH, SALTED/PLA KEM Thais would normally buy this fish — usually a salted grouper or rockfish — in the market. Perhaps it can be made more economically at home. Use any firm, white-fleshed fish (especially good is fish that is a little too old to serve fresh). Rub it with salt (allow 2 tablespoons per 300 g/10½ oz) and then dry out in the oven overnight on the lowest possible setting until the fish is dry. When dried, store in the refrigerator where it will keep for 2 months. To use, rehydrate in water for 10 minutes.

FISH SAUCE/NAM PLA This type of sauce is used in one form or another throughout Southeast Asia. Although similar, varieties are not interchangeable. It is made from small fish or prawns (shrimp) that are salted and fermented in the sun for several months. Often the residue from this fermentation is used to make kapi (shrimp paste), the paste essential to Thai cuisine. Fish sauce is pungently salty and has a piercing aroma, but mellows when combined with other ingredients. There is no substitute, it is widely available and does not deteriorate.

FLOUR, TAPIOCA/BLAENG MAN This is the starch extracted from cassava root. It is a fine white powder, that is most often used in small quantities in Thai desserts to add a chewy texture.

FLOUR, RICE/BLAENG KAO JAO Most commonly used in desserts, it is readily available in Asian food stores.

GALANGAL/KHA Also known as **Laos**. This rhizome is extensively used in Thai cuisine and is now available in most Asian food stores. When young, its skin is creamy white with pink sprouts and is best used in soups, such as Mud Crab Soup. As it matures the skin thickens, the flavour becomes more pungent and peppery and the colour changes to a musty gold — it is then ideal for using in curry pastes, once it has been washed, peeled and shredded. Store it in the refrigerator in a plastic bag to prevent dehydration. If fresh is unavailable, try pickled galangal that has been rinsed then steeped in water sweetened with white (granulated) sugar for 5 minutes. Rinse and drain. To roast galangal, chop, then dry roast in a wok or a pan over a medium heat until it has browned.

GARLIC/GRATIAM Thai garlic is much smaller and less pungent than in the West. The best substitute is young, new season garlic.

When roasting garlic, separate the cloves but leave on the skin. Roast them in a wok with a lid over a medium heat. They are cooked when the exterior is charred. Remove the soft cloves by slicing open the pod and removing the flesh.

To deep-fry, slice the garlic cloves lengthways and deep-fry in safflower oil, stirring regularly for even heat dispersion. Cook until the garlic is a nutty, light golden colour; remove with a slotted spoon and drain on paper towel.

Do not overcook or fry too quickly as they will develop an acrid taste. Deep-fried garlic is wonderful when sprinkled on top of salads or soups.

GINGER/KING Mature (green) ginger is used in soups and in a few curry pastes such as Steamed Chicken Soup and Barramundi with Ginger and Tamarind. Young ginger, with its white and translucent skin and pink sprouts, is used more widely in salads, curries and soups. Buy only firm and unwrinkled rhizomes and store them in a plastic bag or airtight container to prevent dehydration. One way to flavour stocks or soups with ginger and still be able to remove it easily with tongs is by bruising it. Simply crush the required amount with the side of a knife and then add it to a soup such as Steamed Chicken Soup.

GOURDS/FAK LAI CHANIT Thais, like the Chinese, use many types of gourds. None, apart from the bitter gourd, has a very pronounced flavour. They are mainly used for their sponge-like characteristics in soaking up a flavoursome curry. All gourds need to be peeled and well cooked before eating. Cucumbers may be substituted.

JASMINE/MALI HORM Also known as Arabian Jasmine. These buds are steeped in water overnight, then the water is used to make desserts, sweet coconut cream or Perfumed Rice. Rose petals may be substituted.

KAFFIR LIME/MAKRUT The leaves of this citrus fruit garnish curries, salads and soups. They are used extensively throughout the cuisine. Fortunately, fresh leaves are now readily available. Dry or frozen leaves should not be used — they merely add fibre without any of the fragrance that the fresh leaves impart. The trees are also now available, so should access to shops which carry these leaves be inconvenient, buy a tree instead, thus ensuring a ready supply. The fruit is expensive and difficult to obtain, but can be bought frozen. It is usually the zest that is called for in most recipes, and the zest from the frozen fruit is quite satisfactory.

KAPI Also known as shrimp paste. The Thais believe that kapi gives their food its characteristic flavour — certainly excluding kapi from any of the recipes where it is specified results in a dish with far less depth and vibrancy. Kapi is made from very small prawns (shrimp) that have been salted, fermented, drained and then dried in the sun. The outcome is one powerful paste, disturbing at first, but quickly an acquired taste. Thai kapi is different from those of surrounding countries — it is less dry and more fragrant. It is readily available and keeps forever in the refrigerator. Mercifully, it comes in an airtight container. In most recipes it needs to be roasted before using. Either wrap in foil and grill, broil or roast in the oven for 5–10 minutes until it has lost its 'raw' fragrance, or zap in the microwave in a covered bowl for 3–5 minutes. It keeps indefinitely this way too, either inside or outside the refrigerator.

KRACHAI Sometimes known as lesser galangal or rhizome, or Chinese key. It is most often used in jungle curries and with fish. It is only rarely available fresh, but it can be easily purchased pickled in brine. Before using, rinse it then steep in water that has been sweetened with white (granulated) sugar for 5 minutes. Rinse and drain again to remove any chemical tastes.

LEMONGRASS/TAKRAI This blade-like plant is now readily available in the West. It is used in curries and in soups, especially Hot and Sour Soups. This plant is very fibrous, so remove the outer sheaths and green wooden top third before using it. It is easily grown by striking the bulb in water, then planting in a large pot with a tray of water beneath to keep the soil very moist.

LIME/MANAO Thai limes are smaller and a little sweeter than their Western counterparts. Key limes can be used as a substitute. Lemon juice does not impart the same fragrance. It is the last resort, not a satisfactory substitute.

MACE/DAWK JAN The outer sheath of nutmeg, it has a subtler, more elusive taste than nutmeg. It is normally only used in the 'foreign' curries, such as Massaman. It should be dry roasted slowly over a low heat before using. This releases an enticing fragrance that dissipates quickly, so it should be ground and used as soon as possible.

MEKHONG WHISKY Thai men drink it straight, with ice or sometimes diluted with soda water. Be warned — it is rocket fuel. Bourbon is a suitable substitute.

MINT/BAI SARAE NAE Thais nearly always use a very fragrant small-leafed variety, very similar to common garden mint, which can be substituted.

MUSHROOMS/HET Many varieties of mushroom are used in Thai cuisine. The most common is the straw mushroom, **Het Fang**, which is used in soups, salads and curries, where it provides a sweet and nutty taste. It is uncommon in the West, so it is better to use a fresh alternative, such as the oyster mushroom, rather than the canned product. The shiitake mushroom, **Het Horm**, is also used and although available fresh, the Thais prefer to use the dried variety as it has more taste and texture, especially when used in soups or dishes that need prolonged cooking. Cloud's Ear Mushrooms, **Het Huu Nuu**, are used in salads or stir fries. During the Thai rainy season, particularly in the north, the locals gather a lot of wild mushrooms — such as ceps, chanterelles, russulas, which are steamed, grilled, broiled or boiled before being used in salads, soups or *nam priks*.

NAM PLA RA The northern version of fish sauce, it is made from a freshwater mud fish which is fermented with roasted rice for several months. Some Thais like to eat the fermented fish, deep-fried and dressed with finely sliced shallots, chillies and lemongrass. Mostly, however, they prefer to use it as a seasoning. It is readily available in the West — every Asian food store will have it — in small glass jars with pickled gourami written on it. Be prepared for a shock when it is opened. It should be quickly boiled with 500 mL (2 cups/16 fl oz) water, a kaffir lime, 2–3 red shallots and 1 stalk of lemongrass. Simmer until the fish has dissolved, about 30 minutes, then strain it. It is used to season *larps* or northern salads and curries.

NUTMEG/LUUK JAN This is always roasted before use. It needs to be crushed before being roasted to ensure that it cooks evenly and then it must be finely ground before use.

OYSTER SAUCE/NAM MAN HOI An extract of oysters combined with caramel and cornflour (cornstarch), it is used extensively in stir-frying and imparts a deliciously rich taste.

PAK CHII FARANG Sometimes known as long-leafed coriander or saw leaf herb, this uncommon herb may be seen in Vietnamese food stores. It has serrated leaves about 5 cm (2 in) long. It is used in soups and salads, especially *larps*. It is quite delicious, with a succulent taste, not dissimilar to coriander (cilantro), which can be substituted.

PANDANUS LEAVES/BAI TOEI HORM These leaves are used in desserts and occasionally in savoury cooking. Their flavour, released only when subjected to heat, is woody and nutty. Available from Asian food stores. If fresh is unobtainable, then try the frozen leaves. Although they are not as fragrant as the fresh, they are a better alternative than the essence that is available in small glass bottles.

PEANUTS/TUA LII SONG These are used extensively as a garnish for salads and as a base for satay sauces and thick red curries. In a wok, deep-fry the peanuts over a low heat in enough safflower oil to cover for 10 minutes, or until they are golden. Remember to take them out a little before they are ready as they will continue to cook after they have been drained.

PEPPERCORNS/PRIK THAI Thais use only two types of peppercorns: white, as a seasoning, and fresh green, as a garnish in jungle curries and stir-fries. Black peppercorns are very rarely used. Ground white pepper, coriander (cilantro) root and garlic pounded together form one of the oldest and most frequently used seasoning pastes in Thai cuisine — before chillies were introduced by the Portuguese in the sixteenth century, it was the major spice that 'heated' Thai food.

PLA GROP A small dried smoked fish, it is occasionally used in curry pastes or in salads.

If it proves hard to find then substitute smoked trout.

RADISH/HUA PAK GART KAO The fresh radish is often used in soups or sour orange curries. The dried salted type is readily obtainable in Asian food stores and can often be found under the name of salted turnip. It should be washed before use.

RICE/KAO There is no substitute for long-grained Thai jasmine rice, which has an elusive scent. The rice should first be washed in several changes of water. Although this removes some of its nutrients, it gets rid of the dust, dead insects and even, occasionally, bolts. Clean the rice by rubbing it between your hands to remove any husks and starch that may make it gluggy. Place the strained rice in a medium pan and cover with fresh water to 1 finger joint (2.5 cm/1 in) above the level of the rice. The ratio is approximately 3½ cups water to 2½ cups rice. For 4–6 people, use 500 g (1 lb) rice. Do not season with salt. Cover with a tight-fitting lid and bring the rice quickly to the boil, then turn the heat down to very low and cook for 15–20 minutes. Check the rice to test if it is cooked. At this stage, further perfume the rice by burying a pandanus leaf in the pot and allowing it to rest for a further 10 minutes. If the rice is too dry on the top when checking, sprinkle with some warm water and re-cover. If it is too wet, add a little bread to absorb some of the excess water and do not re-cover the pot.

Sticky rice is used extensively in the north and north-east of Thailand and neighbouring countries. This short-grained plump rice is unusual in that it clumps together when cooked. It is delicious and very filling. Sticky rice is steamed rather than boiled. Soak the rice overnight in plenty of water so that it can swell. Rinse in several changes of water, then steam for about 20 minutes or until the rice is tender, being careful to check that the rice in the centre of the steamer is cooked. Do not overcook as it hardens and takes on an unsightly yellow tinge.

RICE, ROASTED/KAO KRUA To roast rice, place the required amount in a pan over a low heat, stirring regularly to prevent scorching. When light golden and fragrant, remove from the heat. Cool, then grind very finely. Either regular jasmine rice or sticky rice can be used. The ground rice deteriorates quickly, so only make enough for what is required. If there are any leftovers, store in the refrigerator to prolong its life.

ROLL CUT To roll cut a vegetable, top and tail it, then slice it at a 45° angle, turn slightly and slice again at a 45° angle. Continue rolling and cutting until the end of the vegetable is reached.

SHALLOTS/HORM TAENG One of the most important vegetables in Thai food. They are used in making curry pastes, with abandon in salads and for perfuming soups. Thai shallots are very similar in taste to normal brown or grey shallots, which can be substituted, but they are light purple to red in colour. They are not uncommon. Large purple onions, finely sliced, may also be substituted in curry pastes.

Roasted shallots add a lovely, smoky dimension to salads or curry pastes. To roast shallots, dry roast the unpeeled shallots in a wok until charred, then peel.

To deep-fry, slice the shallots lengthways. In a wok, heat enough safflower oil to cover, add the shallots and cook, stirring constantly, until they begin to colour. Remove with a slotted spoon and drain on paper towel. They will remain crisp for 2 days. Do not store in the refrigerator as they will go soggy. The strained oil from deep-frying is wonderfully fragrant and may be used for stir-frying.

SHALLOTS, CHINESE/TON HORM These are the same as eschallots, scallions or spring onions.

SOY SAUCE/NAM SIEW Thais mainly use soy sauce in stir-fried dishes. Kecap manis, a sweet, thick, dark soy sauce from Indonesia, perfumed with cassia bark and thickened with palm sugar, is often used in Thai food for its colouring.

Light soy sauce may be used as a vegetarian alternative to fish sauce.

STOCK/NAM STOCK 500 g (1 lb) pork, chicken or duck bones are combined with 1 tablespoon salt, 4 cloves garlic, 3-4 coriander stalks, ½ knob ginger and 2 L (2 qt/3½ pt) water. In a large pan bring all the ingredients to a boil, reduce heat and simmer for 2 hours, skimming often. Strain, allow to cool and skim off the fat. It is used as a moistening agent or as a base for soup, rarely as a flavour in itself.

SUGAR/NAM TAAN The Thais use several types of sugar, including the white (granulated) sugar used in the West. Using castor (superfine) sugar is preferable as it dissolves quickly and thoroughly. Palm sugar, **Nam Taan Pep**, made from the sap of the Palmyra palm, has a rich creamy sweetness that is not too cloying. It keeps well and is easily obtainable. Should the sugar be too hard, then cover it with a little water and heat in the microwave oven for 30–60 seconds, mix in the water and the sugar will remain soft and easy to work with. Another sugar is made from the sugar palm, **Nam Taan Bik**. The flavour is not so complex, but it can be used instead of the Palmyra palm sugar. Finally, there is coconut sugar, **Nam Taan Mapraow**, which is white in colour and mainly used for desserts. It is easily obtainable. Substitute with palm sugar.

TAMARIND/MAKAM SOT or BLIAK Fresh tamarind is an uncommon delight. It is one of the major souring agents in Thai food. It should be firm yet supple, not brittle to the touch, and should be peeled and deseeded before using either in soups or *nam prik*. By far the more common version in the West is in block form. Its taste is not unlike sour prunes or dates. To use it, break off a small block, wash in water, then immerse in warm water for several minutes until softened — use about 3 tablespoons of tamarind to 250 mL (1 cup/8 fl oz) water. The pulp is then squeezed and worked to remove it from the fibres and dissolve it in the water. Finally it is strained. It can be made up to 1 week in advance as long as it is kept in the refrigerator. After this time it may begin to ferment.

TOFU (see Beancurd)

TSIANT/PRESERVED VEGETABLES Made from pickled and salted cabbage and radish, they are used in noodle soups to add flavour. They can be found in Asian food stores in a squat brown stoneware jar.

TURMERIC/KAMIN This rhizome, which is related to ginger, grows throughout South-East Asia. It has a strong, almost medicinal smell and should be used with discretion. Fresh is preferable, but should that not be available, use half the specified quantity of dried ground turmeric. Ensure that the powder is pure turmeric, because the inferior brands often have an acrid taste. White turmeric, **Kamin Kao**, uncommon outside Thailand, is used as a vegetable on *nam prik* or *lon* plates.

VINEGAR/NAM SOM Thais use a white vinegar based on coconut, readily available in the West. Pungent alone, it is quite pleasant when used with other ingredients. Often it can be used in place of lime juice.

WATERCRESS/SIAMESE PAK BUNG Also known as swamp cress or morning glory, it is better known as *kwan tong* or *ong choy*. It is quite delicious and is readily available throughout the summer months in Asian food stores. Spinach may be substituted.

WINE/LAO JIN When wine is occasionally called for, use *shao xing* (Chinese rice wine). Dry sherry is a standard substitute.

WING BEANS/TUA PHUU This is a thick, frilled and succulent bean often used in salads, stir-fried with a little garlic, or used as a vegetable with *nam priks* or *lons*. Substitute asparagus or green beans.

YELLOW BEANS/TOW JIAW A sauce based on fermented yellow soy beans, which is intensely salty and quite delicious. Used in sauces and soups it normally indicates a dish of Chinese origin. The Chinese also have such a sauce, but use the Thai variety instead which is readily available.

INDEX